Congratulations
from

DOUR AZUL

CRUZEIROS

The Douro Princess Crew
Wishes you a Happy Birthday.

MARCH PAST

THE MEMOIRS OF A MAJOR GENERAL

*Molly whose love and support over 57 years
has been my greatest stroke of luck.*

March Past

The Memoirs of a Major General

by

MAJOR GENERAL
SIR BRIAN WYLDBORE-SMITH

The Memoir Club

© Major General Sir Brian Wyldbore-Smith 2001

First published in 2001 by
The Memoir Club
Whitworth Hall
Spennymoor
County Durham

British Library Cataloguing in
Publication Data.
A catalogue record for this book
is available from the
British Library.

ISBN: 1 84104 039 8

Typeset by George Wishart & Associates, Whitley Bay.
Printed by Bookcraft (Bath) Ltd.

To my wife and family

Contents

Illustrations ix

Foreword xi

Introduction xiii

Chapter 1 Early Life 1

Chapter 2 Schooldays 15

Chapter 3 Military Initiation 24

Chapter 4 Egyptian Experiences 30

Chapter 5 The War Continues 37

Chapter 6 Journey Towards Peace 57

Chapter 7 The Aftermath of War 62

Chapter 8 Married Life 74

Chapter 9 Post War Employment 89

Chapter 10 More Military Responsibilities 93

Chapter 11 Settling Down 109

Chapter 12 Grantham House 121

Chapter 13 Brief Business Interlude 126

Chapter 14 A Career in Politics 129

Chapter 15 Margaret Thatcher and Me 138

Chapter 16 The Brighton Bombing 143

Chapter 17 Political Vignettes 149

Chapter 18 An Active Retirement 157

Conclusions 164

Further Reflections 166

Illustrations

Molly . . . . Frontispiece

The author aged 21 with his father and mother   3

The author with ferrets   5

Theatricals at Wynyard   10

The Desert Campaign 1941   38

Italian prisoners at Sidi Barrani   40

Gunner Raine, my driver/batman   42

Helen in the desert   44

German prisoners at Tobruk   52

Map of the Desert Campaign: East of Agheila   55

Map of the Desert Campaign: West of Agheila   56

Map of the 11th Armoured Division Advance in Europe .   63

ACV Team, 11th Armoured Division   65

Montgomery on Rommel   70

Wedding, 1 April 1944, Savoy Chapel   78

Bournehill House   85

Celebrating the author's 80th birthday with family   87

The house at Ipoh   99

House in Nassim Road, Singapore 105

Admiral Sir Varyl Begg and Lord Selkirk 107

Constable's Tower, Dover 110

The author, Bunny Connolly-Carew and Keith Bailey
    at Dover 112

Installation of Sir Robert Menzies as Lord Warden
    of the Cinque Ports 117
Restolho d'Aveia – house in Portugal 119
Grantham House: the author with his dogs 124
Margaret Thatcher at Grantham House 139

Foreword
by Margaret Thatcher

SIR BRIAN WYLDBORE-SMITH'S memoirs reflect, as all good memoirs should, the author's own character – in this case, direct, generous, modest, energetic and witty. His has been a life of active service and it has been conducted from first to last in the style of an English gentleman. At times, Sir Brian reflects sadly and critically upon current social trends. But at least while there are old soldiers still young in spirit – soldiers like him – we may be sure that something remains to inspire the new generation.

At one of the Marquess of Londonderry's Christmas parties, the young Brian was seated next to Field Marshal Sir Henry Wilson, Chief of the Imperial General Staff, who regaled the boy with enthralling tales of the Great War. Just two months later Wilson was assassinated by the IRA. It was from this moment, we learn, that Brian decided to join the army.

In 1933 he received his commission into the Royal Artillery. Wyldbore-Smith served briefly in Palestine. With the outbreak of War, the pace of military life quickened sharply. In the years that followed he and his dogs, and later horses, were despatched from one field of combat to another. In these memoirs, it is of comradeship, amusing incidents and exuberant high spirits that the reader learns most. But they were also years of hardship and danger – as when Wyldbore-Smith was first shot out of a church steeple and then off a telegraph post in an engagement on the Garigliano River, as a result of which he was awarded the DSO.

Brian Wyldbore-Smith's life in the services brought him into close contact with many of the great figures of the time, not least Montgomery into whose personal and professional qualities he offers fascinating insight. But Wyldbore-Smith's memoirs also reveal a life that was always more than one-dimensional. In the descriptions of his beloved wife, his children, his friends, his travelling menagerie of animals, his houses and his gardens, this understated, and so typically English, account again and again comes to life. It is a distinctive and, I think, extremely healthy feature of the military tradition of this country that our soldiers should be human beings, not mere automata. This was a very human soldier's life.

In the years since leaving the army, these qualities were put to excellent use by the Conservative Party, for which Sir Brian became one of the key fund-raisers. Political fund-raising is one of those activities for which high-minded people often, particularly nowadays, express some disdain. But without it, we would all be dependent on the state, and democracy itself would be the loser. And keeping our democracy – our way of life, our rights and our liberties – safe is what Major General Sir Brian Wyldbore-Smith and others have bravely, willingly, joyfully done. These memoirs are part of our island story.

Introduction

THIS IS NOT A MILITARY or political history. It does, I hope, give some of the backdrop, atmosphere and descriptions of people with whom I have been associated over sixty years, first in the army and then with the Conservative Party. Some of these people are well known but many are men and women of all ranks whom I am privileged to call friends.

Throughout my life I have been blessed with good health and good luck, a happy childhood and good friends. I joined the army at the right time, just six years before the war. I survived the war and have been associated with many people who have made their mark in the army, in politics, or simply in life in general.

I decided to commit my life to paper in this way for several reasons. If it was to serve no other purpose than to make clear the events of the last decades in my own mind then it would still have been a worthwhile undertaking. Having lived so long and experienced so much I wanted to look back through the events of my life and writing this memoir has allowed me to do just that. I was also encouraged by enthusiastic family and friends, particularly my wife Molly, to leave something behind me as they believed that I have an interesting story to tell. The composition of this work has certainly satisfied my own desires to look back upon my life and career and will hopefully satisfy the desires of the reader also.

CHAPTER 1

Early Life

BORN IN 1913, the second son of a country vicar in County Durham, I was fortunate to be brought up in a family, which, although without any of the advantages of wealth or rank, was extremely happy. My family was one of the Smiths of Exeter, with a record which goes back over five hundred years, producing more parsons in Dorset than there are churches!

My parents met in June 1905 at Grantham House, their names being the first entries in the visitors book. My mother was the daughter of George Green, a brewer. Through her mother she was also connected with the Sedgwicks of Sedgwick Breweries who bought Grantham House in 1854. This first meeting must have been a successful one as there is another entry in the same visitors book for the following year. This second entry tells of the Reverend and Mrs Wyldbore-Smith, who were married earlier in the year, staying at the house together for the first time as man and wife. Their marriage introduced some good, healthy blood into what was a rather old and inbred family, but unfortunately with no money – George Green had spent it as rapidly as he had earned it. At the time of their engagement my father was a humble curate living and working in Henley on Thames. Shortly after meeting my mother he was awarded his first living at Shalburn near Hungerford.

My parents started a family shortly after being married

but their first child, a daughter, was stillborn in 1907. Though this must have been very upsetting for both my mother and my father their disappointment was alleviated when my brother was born in 1909. In 1912 my parents and brother moved to Thorpes Thewles in the north east of England and here they remained until 1927. After the move my arrival in the world completed our little family

Our family life was extremely happy. My mother was a strong character who provided the driving force behind my father, a man of great charm but lacking in drive and ambition. I believe he could well have become a bishop had he shown more initiative and enterprise. They moved in every social circle and treated everyone with respect and kindness, irrespective of their background. This perhaps accounts for their tremendous popularity and the respect they commanded in the local area. My mother in particular was always friendly and helpful to anyone who approached her and was well liked because of this.

My father was six foot tall, good looking and possessing great charm. He had a fine baritone voice. In fact, when the D'Oyle Carte Opera Company came to Stockton-on-Tees they would frequently call upon him to fill a vacancy if it occurred. He was easy going and relied on his charm rather than his personality. My mother, on the other hand, was very strong willed with a vibrant personality and the ability to get on with anyone.

I always enjoyed a good relationship with my mother, father and brother and our family life was an extremely happy and stable one. Looking back I can see that, though neither parent was particularly demonstrative, both were immensely fond of one another as well as having a great deal of love and affection for their two children. They always

The author aged 21 with his father and mother.

seemed to have plenty of time to take in activities with me and my brother – expeditions to Stockton-on-Tees in the dog cart, tobogganing and skating in the winter and walks in the country with my father when he went visiting his parishioners. My mother was a very good influence upon me and I spent a lot of time with her before going away to school. She taught me to cook, garden and milk the goats as well as encouraging my love of nature and animals. In the summer evenings the family would play games in the garden and in winter it would be a game of cards around the table. How lucky we were compared to children of this day and age, whose parents are too busy to spend time with their children, apart from perhaps an hour or so in the evenings.

I also enjoyed a good relationship with my brother Tony, who was four years my senior. We were very good friends for the first eight years of my life in particular and spent a great deal of time together before we both started school. Though we got on well together we were very different in terms of character with me being the more confident, curious and gregarious brother whilst Tony was more reserved and guarded. Much leisure time was spent shooting with our Winchester 2.2s, ferreting and, in later years, he would take me in his motorbike and sidecar to the local ferret shows where we would exhibit our pets. I was very attached to my ferrets and used to supplement their diet of bread and milk with sparrows, which we shot off the roofs and haystacks in the village. The inhabitants were very long-suffering and seemed to put up with us in a way which would never occur today. At prep school, however, we were very competitive and I think it a very good thing that our parents then sent us to different public schools.

We were encouraged to mix with all the inhabitants of the

The author with ferrets.

village and had many friends amongst the children of the local school. Indeed, we were positively encouraged to mix with the local children and my friends were the children of farmers and shopkeepers. At weekends, my brother and I would go for walks in the country with other children of our age. We also saw a good deal of the Townsend children, whose parents were friends of the family, and would visit the Londonderry children at Christmases and Easter.

My parents were animal lovers and I cannot remember a time when we were without pets of some kind. At Thorpe Thewles we had a plethora of animal companions – dogs, ferrets, goats, poultry, horses and a pony. I loved to help look after them and regarded this as a pleasure rather than a chore. Many of the animals were domestic pets and I remember distinctly a dog called Pax belonging to my mother. She also kept dachshunds for hunting, one of which was unfortunately killed by a train. The house was surrounded by farms and I would often help the farmers in the summer months. I remember riding on the hay wagons as they trundled through the fields, something which I enjoyed greatly.

My earliest memory was of 'Monk', a black cocker spaniel of whom I was very fond. He kept me in order if I plagued him with too much attention and developed the unfortunate habit of collecting eggs from the greenhouse and eating them! My mother tried to cure him of this by filling the eggs with mustard, which he considered very unfair. I remember one Sunday when we were all in church for the morning service and my father was in mid-sermon, Monk walked up the aisle with one of the eggs in his mouth and I was hastily despatched by Mother to lead him out.

As well as being Vicar of Grindon, my father was

Chaplain to the Seventh Marquess of Londonderry. He and his wife Edith, the Marchioness, lived in Wynyard Park. The Hall was a magnificent Palladian building standing in about 200 acres, with the loveliest gardens, a lake, cricket ground and 3000 acres of land. The Hall itself contained a statue gallery, a dining room capable of seating fifty people, a private chapel and endless reception rooms, looked after by a staff of well over thirty. In addition to Wynyard Park, the Marquess owned Londonderry House in Park Lane and Mount Stewart in Northern Ireland, on the shores of Loch Strangford. However, it was at Wynyard Park that they spent Christmas and much of the shooting season and where they entertained extensively.

As well as conducting services in the private chapel my father also looked after the household and was required to be present in his official capacity at many of the functions. He conducted the marriage service of their eldest daughter, Maureen, to Oliver Stanley, in Durham Cathedral in the early twenties. It was a great occasion, which I attended at the age of eight.

Edith Londonderry became a great friend of my mother's and was also my godmother. They were extremely generous and we received many benefits; I remember that we always had coal in unlimited quantities from their Seaham Colliery. We also had fodder for the horse and were taken by the Londonderry cars to Stockton Races on many occasions. During the Christmas holidays we spent much time at Wynyard. They had four daughters and a son. The latter was somewhat older than my brother and two of the daughters were my age. Like many families of the aristocracy, the children were brought up by Nanny in the nursery and only saw their parents in the mornings and evenings. I spent much time in the nursery with them. Nanny Stevenson was a great favourite of us all and many were the times I spent the afternoons there and was sent down to see Lady Londonderry with her children at tea-time.

As I said, the Londonderrys had four daughters and a son – Maureen, Margaret, Helen, Mary and Robin. Mary is the only surviving Londonderry and is now Lady Bury. Robin was the same age as my brother and attended Eton. I remember him getting sent down for a term as he had been caught smoking and he was sent to stay with us for the duration of his exclusion. Robin looked a lot like his mother but was something of a weak character whilst the girls were stronger and more ambitious. In later life he almost disappeared from society when he went to live in Devon but the Londonderry name has been preserved by his children.

Lord Londonderry was also very generous in helping my parents financially. When I managed to get an Exhibition to Wellington College but the only vacancy was in a house and not the college itself, which cost an extra £35 a year, Lord Londonderry paid the £35.

At Christmas there were the most wonderful parties. My mother and father, my brother and I used to get into the wagonette, my father would harness up the horse, and we would travel the four miles to Wynyard Hall. There we would be received at the portico of the Palladian hall by the butler, Mr Stribling, and once inside we divested ourselves of all our outdoor clothes and were ushered into one of the reception rooms. The Christmas dinner was always a great occasion. Probably thirty or forty would sit down to the meal with a footman behind every other chair. Before it we would assemble in a large anteroom and a footman would come round with a salver with a number of envelopes on it.

Each gentleman would be given an envelope, inside which was the name of the lady he was to escort into dinner.

I remember that in about 1921, at the age of eight, I opened mine to find inside the Marchioness of London-derry's name, and when the piper arrived, off we went in to dinner – me aged eight, with Lady Londonderry on my right arm! She was quite charming to children and talked to them always as if they were grown-ups.

At another Christmas gathering, I had sitting next to me Field Marshal Sir Henry Wilson, who was then the Chief of the Imperial General Staff. He gave me exciting accounts of life during the Great War, which completely fascinated me. Two months after this he was shot by the IRA outside his house in London and I remember writing to Lady Wilson, probably at the instigation of my mother, commiserating with her on her loss. She wrote back to me a most charming letter, which I still have. It was from this moment that I was determined to join the army. This proved to be a cataclysmic turning point in my life and I do not remember ever wavering in my decision to become part of the great British military.

The parties at the Londonderry mansion were indeed legendary and vast numbers of men would assemble to go shooting. As Lady Londonderry was a flamboyant and dramatic personality she would always organise some theatrical event during the festive period. These would usually take place over three nights and the estate workers would attend the performance on the opening night whilst the second two nights were rather drunken and lively. Many of the guests were very amusing and entertaining and Lady Londonderry always invited a professional actor to stay and coach those who were in the performance. Amongst those

Theatricals at Wynyard. Author 3rd from left in back row.

who fulfilled this role were Sir Headley Williamson and Ena Grossmith.

I also remember Princess Helena Victoria, the daughter of Queen Victoria, coming to stay. People did not take very good care of their teeth in those days and she had one huge tooth which I found quite remarkable. After having been introduced to her at the dinner table I turned to my mother and said, 'Isn't that tooth extraordinary!' Obviously this did not go down terribly well but I find it to be quite amusing in retrospect.

Wynyard was a most beautiful place and it always seemed to be filled with the most beautiful flowers. There was a stunning statue gallery in the building also and one could walk round its balcony. Robin gave my brother and me a guided tour of this gallery and pointed out all the ruder features of the statues! They had a very famous racing stallion too which we would observe grazing in its paddock.

The building now belongs to John Hall who was a Tory patron. He has restored it to something of its former state including the restoration of the magnificent thirty-seater dining room and the wonderful grapevines. John's father was a miner at a colliery in Seaham which had belonged to the Londonderry estate.

When the lake at Wynyard froze over in the winter, which it frequently seemed to do, we used to play ice hockey and Lady Londonderry, who was immensely fit and active, loved organising hockey matches. We would also have matches on their cricket ground where we would get up a team and play against a side raised by the Londonderry children.

Each New Year's eve there was a party similar to the one held at Christmas. I remember one occasion, a dinner attended by the usual thirty or forty people. We all went into an enormous drawing room where a great silver salver of sultanas swimming in brandy (known as 'snapdragon') was set alight. We then had bravely to put a hand into the fire, pull out a sultana and eat it. After this came what was known as the 'bell game'.

Lady Londonderry would tell everyone to shut their eyes and to stay at one end of the room. Then, seizing an enormous bell, she would race off out of the room and up the staircase, ringing the bell loudly. The bell could be heard getting softer and softer as she reached the far end of the hall and once it could no longer be heard everyone rushed out to try to find her. Those who found her had to hide with her and the last person to find her was the loser. Such was the size of the house that quite frequently children used to get lost and the ensuing hour would then be spent trying to recover them from the various bedrooms or attics into which they had strayed.

Not only did we spend much of the Christmas holiday at Wynyard but also, at Easter, we were invited to Mount Stewart for ten days. This was another Palladian house on the shores of Loch Strangford; not as large as Wynyard but with a lake, boats and fishing. We would go sailing on the loch and collect terns' eggs from the 365 islands in the loch. A frequent guest there was Edmund Brock, the artist, who used to teach my mother to paint in lacquer, and I still have the small boxes which she decorated under his guidance.

My early days followed a fairly standard pattern and I was well established in a routine. I would rise at around 7.30 and at 8 the family would gather together for prayers in the dining room. This would include any domestic staff who were in our employ at the time. Our main help around the home was a girl called Annie Langhorn who stayed with the family for fifteen years and who was regarded very much as a family member. The prayers would last for approximately ten minutes and each member of the family was given a prayer pamphlet to read. Unfortunately, we were one short and I was seven when I discovered that my version was German grammar. I was so disgruntled by this incident that I refused ever to attend prayers again!

After breakfast I would have lessons with a governess for the whole of the morning with a short break in the garden. Lunch was followed by a walk in the countryside or games on the lawn. This enabled me to become very familiar with the natural world and aided my general education a great deal. Evenings were free and would usually be spent with the family or looking after the animals.

On Sunday mornings we had to attend matins at the church. Luckily, my mother always encouraged my father to preach only short sermons so the services were not too dull. I especially liked the music and the church had a very good choir and organist. In the afternoons I usually had to attend Sunday school. Despite a fairly religious upbringing I never had any desire to follow in my father's professional footsteps and my mother actively discouraged me from becoming a parson.

At the end of the war my brother went off to preparatory school. I then had a governess who used to come daily to Thorpe Thewles to give me lessons in the morning and then take me out for walks in the country in the afternoons. She was a wonderful woman by the name of Miss Rogers, (though she was affectionately known as Roddy) and lived at 99 Parliament Street, Stockton on Tees, coming out to our house every day on the train. She was a remarkable spinster and taught me well, except for writing; unfortunately she taught me script in which you never join the letters together. In consequence, to this day I have great difficulty in writing in a legible hand.

However, she was wonderful on the walks and encouraged in me an interest in natural history. We would find tadpoles and frogs, collect butterflies, identify birds and learn the names of every plant and flower. Additionally, she taught and encouraged good manners and etiquette and had a great effect upon my life, being with me between the ages of four and nine. I shall always remember her fondly.

Chapter 2

Schooldays

IN 1921, I joined my brother Tony at his preparatory school, Meadowcroft, on the shores of Lake Windermere. It was a very happy school, run by an Australian called Mr Daniel who lived on the premises with his wife and daughter (a girl known as Bubby perhaps due to the fact that she was so well endowed!). I think this period played a greater part in my education than any other school or establishment I subsequently attended. Here I learned to enjoy learning.

The school was quite a modern building and boasted charming gardens and an excellent cricket field. The lake also provided a perfect swimming pool and we were taught to swim round the pier with a brace fixed to our shoulders and a master on the shore holding us up. Swimming lessons took place in the summer mornings during a break between lessons. Despite the fact that it was summer, I remember the water being very cold!

Our location meant that weekends were spent walking in the Lake District and I cultivated a real love and under-standing of this picturesque region. I have been back to the Lake District in later years and found the landscape to be just as pleasing as it was in my schooldays. We were often taken into the hills by coach for walking expeditions which I very much enjoyed. Our proximity to the lake meant that we could go out boating and practise fishing.

I adjusted quickly to life in this friendly school and the

transitionary period was perhaps eased by the fact that my brother was there too. Indeed, I do not recall any bullying having taken place, either by masters or by other boys. The other boys were friendly and were mostly the sons of professional men from the north east of England or children of the landed gentry. I had many friends whom I would invite to stay at the vicarage in the school holidays.

As one would expect, a sensible routine was employed and we would rise at 7 a.m. and have prayers in the lecture hall. After breakfast we would have lessons for three hours until lunch and lessons would again resume in the afternoon. The curriculum was fairly broad though I do not remember learning any modern languages during my time there. The German teacher was unpopular, possibly because the war was still so fresh in the mind of the nation and many of the masters had actually fought in it, and was referred to as 'The Hun'. However, I enjoyed and excelled at both Greek and Latin as the teacher was very competent. I also liked history and mathematics and found the lessons stimulating and interesting. The discipline at the school was benevolent and reasonable and I do not recall having ever found myself in serious trouble.

School sports were always fun and we would have a sports day which the parents would also attend. The masters encouraged sport and gave out medals to reward the boys, whether they had done particularly well or not. On one occasion I was awarded a cup for performing brilliantly in the long jump. I was very pleased as were my parents.

There was a remarkable master called Mr Badger who got me deeply interested in the classics. He was also a great games man and gave me excellent coaching in cricket. He was a young man, about twenty three years old, who had been recently demobbed and was a great classicist and athlete. He taught very well indeed and also encouraged us enjoy games and physical activities. It was due to him and the general atmosphere here that I learned to appreciate not only this school but also Wellington College, to which I went five years later. My parents invited him to come to stay for a week or so during each of the holidays, in order to improve my cricket. I remember putting up a net on the lawn at the vicarage and Mr Badger bowling at me for hours on end to improve my strokes.

My worst day at the school took place one Sunday. My brother and I were walking in the country and he was taking pictures with a new camera he had been given. Seeing a snake on the ground he picked it up the better to take its picture. Unfortunately, this snake transpired to be an adder which bit his wrist as he picked it up. We then had to race back to the school so he could receive medical attention. I was exceedingly worried and frightened at the time but immensely relieved when he recovered from the bite.

School in those days was very different from what it is now. Not only was there only one half term and we did not come home practically every weekend as they do now, but the fees were very much less. Although £300 per term was a great deal of money in those days, the education was excellent and I do not think the policy of corporal punishment administered both by masters and senior prefects at public schools in those days did anyone very much harm.

After Meadowcroft I went on to Wellington College to spend a very happy four years under the headmastership of a Mr Malim, who was an outstanding headmaster. There was considerable competition to get a place at Wellington with around three to four hundred boys competing for only eighty places. The atmosphere there was not particularly military but the emphasis upon the corps was probably greater then (1927-31) than it is now. The corps was an army class which contained around half the sixth form students. I very much enjoyed being part of it, starting off as a private and finishing as a sergeant major. Indeed, the pleasure I derived from the army was probably due to the fact that it was very much a continuation of my education.

The college was granted its Royal Charter in 1853 as the 'Royal and Religious Foundation of The Wellington College' and was opened in 1859 as a national memorial to the great Duke of the same name. It was established in order to provide a high level of education to the young men of the surrounding areas. Since then the college had grown and expanded and pupils from many different areas came to study at the school as boarders. It aimed not only to educate boys like myself in the usual curriculum but also to encourage individuals to strive to be honest, just and to excel in all endeavours, however minor. Additionally, we were encouraged to maintain impeccably high standards of conduct and to be loyal and dignified, the motto of the college being *Lumen Accipe et Imperti* (receive the light and pass it on).

Wellington College was an ornate brick building which stood in 400 acres of magnificent woodland. All the buildings that were used as classrooms and dormitories as well as the houses in which some boys lived and the splendid playing fields were on one campus. There were the usual dormitories as well as five houses in the grounds and I occupied one of these when I attended the college. All the houses and dormitories were named after famous army generals and I was in Wellesley house. This was actually fifteen minutes walk from the main building and so I became very fit walking to and from lessons. Though we did have to concentrate upon our academic studies, sport was given quite a lot of emphasis at Wellington and we engaged in games of cricket and rugby as well as swimming in the excellent pool. Extra-curricular activities of this kind seemed to be very important and the education we received was well balanced.

The atmosphere in the house in which I lived was very homely and I got on well with the thirty boys from my house. Most of the masters too were very convivial and I again enjoyed history and maths lessons, the teachers being particularly good. My closest friends were Roger Bushell, Jack Bates and Anthony Lovibond. I remember one amusing incident when Lovibond acquired some cocktails which we proceeded to consume. Lovibond himself got awfully tight and we had terrible trouble getting him into chapel without letting the masters see how drunk he was!

At Wellington College we participated in military activities including drill, turnout dressing, marching and shooting. We also took part in summer camps with other schools such as Eton and Rugby. We slept on straw mattresses in the open air which was very different. The camps were tremendous fun and we would have games as well as engaging in a little military activity. This largely consisted of infantry tactics and the digging of trenches, similar to those used in World War 1. Sometimes boys would get injured in these activities but never very seriously. Some of the masters had fought in this war and helped with the corps activities. We would also meet boys from other schools on these camps which was quite exciting.

During this time I studied the classics and was probably

the last person to enter the army on a classical education. I suppose I was gregarious and liked communal life. Fagging was the fashion. I was house fag to a boy called Roger Bushell (who became one of my closest friends), the Head of House, a school prefect and captain of the school rugger fifteen – almost a god as far as I was concerned! When I had mumps and was in the sanatorium for ten days he visited me and then wrote to my parents to say how I was progressing.

Being a fag was a fairly usual thing in those days and it involved looking after the senior boy and attending to his needs. I would have to wake him in the morning with a cup of tea, make his bed, tidy his room and bring him tea and toast in the afternoon. Other activities included doing his domestic chores and his shopping and cleaning his shoes. Later I was a fag for a boy called Foster, with whom I would later go shooting. I had to take his clothes to the laundry and remember getting a terrible verbal lashing for leaving his cufflinks in his shirts!

As a captain in the war, Roger Bushell was captured in Italy and sent to a Stalag, where he organised escapes. Under his leadership the prisoners built three tunnels known as Tom, Dick and Harry. Two of the tunnels were discovered but Harry was completed and about seventy officers escaped through it, Roger being the last to do so. Most of them were recaptured before they reached Switzerland. Roger was caught and identified as the organiser, taken into a wood and shot in the back of the head by a Nazi storm trooper. There was a very powerful BBC documentary made of this episode entitled 'Behind the Bars'.

At sixteen I took the examinations known as the School Certificate and passed in five or six subjects. The papers were in subjects such as English and history and I seem to remember them being rather difficult. Before leaving Wellington at eighteen one took the Higher Certificate and this time I passed three subjects. Now I was ready to continue my military based education in Woolwich Military Academy.

The Royal Military Academy at Woolwich was the equivalent of Sandhurst for those desiring to become officers in the Royal Engineers or the Royal Artillery. The Woolwich examination took place over two days in the Burlington Gallery, London. It consisted of eight papers and was, as far as I remember, rather hard. Again, competition for places was intense and I was one of fifty bright and lucky enough to gain a place at the Academy. The course I would take was to last eighteen months during which time we would be trained in the ways of the military.

The syllabus consisted of military history, physical activities, games, mathematics and some night training. In many ways, it was very similar to a university consisting of an eighteen-month course and in the first six months I was a 'snooker' and counted for nothing. In the second six months I was an 'intermediate' and during the last six months a 'senior'. Seniors had more responsibility and were often placed in charge of the juniors during their first term. I liked this taste of authority and found that it suited me quite well.

Lessons at Woolwich were taught in very much the same way as they were at school. The masters used a blackboard and lectured to the class but some lessons, such as map-reading, were held outside, which was much more interesting. Life was rather hectic and I was certainly never bored. We started the day at 6.30 and were kept busy with lessons until lunch after which we enjoyed games. The evenings were filled with studies and homework. A week at the end of each term was set aside for tactical training and we were then trained in artillery, tactics, leadership and man management. Lectures by senior officers such as the Chief of General Staff and members of the Army Council were also given.

The discipline in the college was strict but I did not object to this at all. Indeed, I think discipline is a very good thing and feel that there should be more of it in our educational establishments, not less. Black marks were given for misdemeanours and if an individual amassed too many he would have to run round the college in his pyjamas.

Whilst at 'The Shop' I enjoyed the hospitality of numerous hostesses who were launching their daughters on the Season. I used to attend dances in London, travelling by tram from Woolwich to the West End in my tailcoat and returning by the same transport by six o'clock in the morning. We would have to get changed on the trams which added to the air of excitement. Though Woolwich was obviously a male institution many of the students at Woolwich had sisters and their parents would ask us boys to go and be their dancing partners. This kind of behaviour was tolerated but if you were caught you were given a number of days 'hoxter', which meant getting up at six and running around the grounds – about one mile – before breakfast. I am sure that I benefited greatly from this participation in the social whirlwind and had a good deal of fun but very little sleep!

The living conditions were relatively good and we slept in old fashioned barrack rooms, eight to each room. There was not a great deal of furniture, only a bed, a desk and somewhere to put our clothes. In addition, there was a common room in which we could socialise. There was an internal social life at Woolwich (as well as the unofficial nights out and weekends spent at home) which largely consisted of having dinner and drinks with the company commander. Additionally, there would be one guest night per month for which we dressed up and drank beer. A strange ritual also took place during which the seniors would chase the juniors round the college.

The top fifteen graduates were posted to the Royal Engineers. I was sixteenth and therefore became a Gunner. This was probably a fortunate solution, as I have always regarded Sappers as mad, Methodists and married! I was not in the least perturbed by my performance and have often thought how lucky I was to become a Gunner rather than a Sapper. This former occupation proved to be much more fun and involved a great deal of action as I was soon to discover.

CHAPTER 3

Military Initiation

IN 1933 I RECEIVED my commission into the Royal Artillery and proceeded to Lark Hill. Here young officers learned the skills of gunnery, firing 18 pounder guns and driving the horses that drew the guns, as wheel driver, centre driver and lead driver. After six months I arrived at the 18th Field Regiment, stationed at Brighton, a fully-fledged gunner officer. Brighton was a wonderful place to be at this time and I was very lucky in my first posting. It was a great introduction to the Royal Regiment of Artillery and, indeed, to the army – a horse-drawn regiment, pleasant social life, hunting with the South Down Hounds and polo in Preston Park.

There were many splendid social amenities in Brighton and the dance halls, though otherwise quite similar to those frequented by young people today, were free of violence and drugs. In those days we were slow to develop and at the age of nineteen I was comparatively innocent. Brighton – Sherry's dance hall on Saturday nights and the local fillies – soon completed my education! Sherry's was a nightclub typical of this time. It was very big and held old fashioned dances which required a partner – very different to the modern dances of today. There would be lots of girls sitting on seats which went right round the perimeter of the dance hall and the young men would approach them and ask them to dance. It was all very innocent really despite the lack of chaperones and one did not even have much to drink. The girls would be very well turned out whilst the men would be smart and had to wear a suit.

I had sixteen soldiers under my command and found them to be easy to relate to and fun to work with. They were all in good shape as there was a great emphasis upon physical activity. Most of the soldiers were from country backgrounds and had signed on for four to nine years in the regiment. I found that the majority remained for the whole 21 years and were successful. These soldiers were aged between eighteen and forty, the older men having served in the First World War. I had much admiration for these men and treated them with the utmost respect. We participated in a great many tasks together and learned with one another. I also had to teach the soldiers some of the skills I had learned at Woolwich, including mathematics and map-reading.

The routine at Brighton was well established and I soon became accustomed to it. We began with rough exercise followed by breakfast. We then had to clean harness, participate in gun drill, attend a lecture and then have lunch. After a brief period of leisure we would engage in games for the afternoon and the evenings were free time during which we could do what we wished.

At this time we used the 18 pounder which was later replaced by the 25 pounder. This was a much more effective weapon and fired shrapnel, having a 12,000 yard range and firing 6 rounds per minute. I found it to be both effective and accurate. We did a good deal of shooting at Brighton and were taught how to fire properly. We also practised firing barrage with the gun position officer and sometimes shot at moving targets. For signalling, we used the telephone line, semaphore and Morse code as no wireless had yet been introduced.

Each year there were manoeuvres in a camp held on the Sussex downs when we lived in tents and were involved in practical exercises. It was the manoeuvring procedures which the soldiers found most enjoyable. The infantry, who were mostly territorials, were often employed too. We had quite a lot of contact with the Sussex Yeomanry and I got on very well with them throughout the proceedings. I was lucky enough to enjoy a good social life both inside and outside the army at this time and hunted with friends in Sussex as well as engaging in the usual social activities.

The discipline at Brighton was more relaxed than it had been at Wellington. Soldiers did misbehave at times, the most common misdemeanours being drunkenness and debauchery. If they were late returning to the barracks then punishments would be carried out. Depending on the seriousness of the offence and the previous behaviour of the soldier, he would be confined to barracks, court-martialled or detained. The same punishment system applied to the officers.

I look back on my time at Brighton as being a very happy period of my life and one which I enjoyed very much. The town was new and exciting to me, I had many friends and lovely pursuits, the soldiers were friendly and competent and I got on well with my fellow officers. Additionally, I continued to learn about military life and this prepared me well for later events.

After Brighton I moved to Deepcut and lived in huts built for use during World War 1. The accommodation was bad and the surroundings were unpleasant and unattractive. Aldershot was the nearest town and was dominated by the military. My duties here involved keeping the regiment amused (a much harder task than one might at first assume) with concerts, summer games and quizzes. Luckily, my next posting was to be much more enjoyable.

In 1936 I was posted to the Coastal Artillery in Northern Ireland near Loch Swilly. This posting was considered the lowest grade, thanks to the fact that firstly it was Coastal Artillery and secondly it had the worst reputation of any station in the Royal Artillery. A lot of people hated the place and turned to drink in order to deal with the boredom and isolation. The Commanding Officer had been arrested for drunkenness and urinating in public in Londonderry and the powers-that-be decided that its reputation must be restored. They therefore despatched Frank Weldon, later to become the famous equestrian who built the Badminton course, Ian Graeme, later to become leader of the Royal Artillery Skiing Association, and me, to boost morale and improve the reputation of the regiment.

This we duly did by organising activities to keep the men occupied. Again, this was not terribly easy in such an isolated place but we managed it somehow. We kept the men busy by laying on boats to take them fishing and encouraging them to go mountaineering in the austere hills of Ireland. Indeed, the situation changed so much that Loch Swilly soon became a popular posting.

I arrived with a horse, which I hunted and raced in Donegal. Fort Dunree had two nine-inch guns, which were meant to defend Loch Swilly, the harbour for the Grand Fleet in World War 1. It took us some time to discover the art of firing these weapons, which were on the top of a 300-foot hill. In the meantime we made our presence felt by racing, hunting and shooting snipe and also improving relations with the locals. I cannot recall any obvious political tensions at the time and there were no major incidents to speak of.

When engaging in military practice we used 9.2 guns from World War 1 and had a limited number of shells. In fact, ammunition was in such short supply that we were only permitted to fire twelve shells each year which was quite an event. They had a range of twenty miles and were reasonably effective.

One of my friends out there was Pat Herdman, Master of the Strabane Harriers. In 1936, whilst serving at Fort Dunree I was invited over to Mount Stewart in December. It was then probably ten years since I had seen the Londonderry family, either in Ireland or at Wynyard Park. I motored over there and found a large house party assembled for woodcock shooting. Ribbentrop, the German Ambassador to the UK, was staying with his wife. I remember that in the evening at the end of the usual dinner party, Lord Londonderry got up and toasted Hitler, to which Ribbentrop rose and gave the Nazi salute. I thought nothing of this at the time, not, of course, realising what the future held.

Going to Northern Ireland was a great experience for me. I had never visited the country before and found it to be a place of extreme natural beauty. Loch Swilly and Donegal are amongst the most picturesque and serene places in Ireland and I will always remember them. Although there was not much social life and Londonderry, the nearest town, wasn't particularly pleasant, I enjoyed wildlife and shooting as well as entertaining the regiment. The position, which was something of a challenge, appealed to me and I felt gratified that we managed to raise the morale of the men and turn this once loathed place into a popular posting.

I have been back to Loch Swilly in more recent years and visited the fort I helped to transform which is now occupied by Irish soldiers. My daughter Penelope married Pat Herdman's son James and now lives very happily in the area.

CHAPTER 4

Egyptian Experiences

As A RESULT OF OUR SUCCESS in raising the morale at Fort
Dunree, I was given a 'jacket' in 1937. This meant that I
was posted to the Royal Horse Artillery in Egypt – the corps
elite of the Gunners. This entailed some extra expenditure
over and above our pay and I was expected to enter into a
number of activities such as polo or hunting. In those days
the salary of a second lieutenant was ten shillings and
sixpence a day! I remember my mother saying that she
would help by subsidising my finances by four pounds a
month. This seems very little now but it should be
remembered that my father's stipend was about £700 a year.

I arrived in Egypt in October 1937, after a very educational trip on a troopship in the company of three young
officers of my age – Tommy Pitman of the 11th Hussars,
George Murray-Smith of the 7th Hussars and Cavanagh
Mainwaring, a very wild naval officer. The voyage took ten
days during which I rapidly learned to drink, gamble and
generally enjoy myself, arriving in Alexandria with a
monstrous hangover!

I was absolutely fascinated by Egypt but at Abbassia my
reception from the regiment was cool. They had reserva-
tions as to whether I was the right calibre for the RHA and I
was informed by my battery commander, Keith Dunn, that I
could only wear the coveted ball buttons of the Horse
Artillery when I had proved myself. 'Proving oneself'

involved being able to run the troops well, merge well into the existing team and excel at sport, namely polo.

The 3rd Regiment of the RHA had just reached the final of the Cavalry Polo Tournament and was due to play the final against the 8th Hussars that afternoon. My first job was to find one of our team who had disappeared the night before, following a visit to a night-club; his name was Toc Elton, and he later joined the 8th Hussars. He was still missing and due to appear on the polo field at Gazireh that afternoon. Friz Fowler, my battery commander, told me to go out with a more experienced subaltern to try to locate him. I remember that we drove around a variety of night haunts and eventually located Toc in bed with a charming Egyptian dancer, his collarbone broken! We got him back to barracks, a doctor bandaged his left arm so that he could hold the reins and he duly took his place on the polo ground. The 3rd Regiment RHA won the inter regimental tournament and I was congratulated for my part in the victory.

One of the members of this winning team was Friz Fowler, a wonderful horseman and an international polo player with a handicap of seven. I was very fortunate to serve with him. He was a wonderful trainer of both men and horses and will appear frequently in my story, as during the war we served together on many occasions.

In the desert we played a good deal of sport and were fond of cricket, tennis, polo, squash, shooting quail and swimming. These were activities in which the soldiers as well as the officers engaged. As the climate was so different from that of England, we had to be wary of the hot sun. Everyone had to wear a helmet at all times to avoid sunstroke – a measure that seems somewhat antiquated today.

Indeed, to allow yourself to be sunburned was considered to be an offence as it was regarded as a self-inflicted injury.

Again the accommodation was old fashioned but quite pleasant. There was a nice officers' mess which boasted fans and a garden. The soldiers occupied barrack rooms, twelve men to each room. The working day too was much like the one I had grown used to at Brighton and began with exercises in the desert, acting as part of a larger formation, regular meals and training. We also became involved in exercises with other cavalry regiments as this was around the time when General Hobart was mechanising the army. The mechanisation went down well with the soldiers but was met with distrust and suspicion by the officers who regretted the loss of the horses.

Later that year I was sent to Palestine with D Battery of the 3rd Regiment RHA in the role of catching Arabs, who at that time were attacking the Jewish population. A Palestinian policeman was assigned to help us, ensure co-operation and provide intelligence. I got on well with him but always felt rather sorry for the Arabs as it was, after all, their country and it can be argued that the Jews infringed upon them rather than vice versa. Nevertheless, it was not safe to go out alone at night as a wandering Arab would kill first and ask questions later. Additionally, I met the Jewish Zionists who were very friendly and grateful for the help that we were providing but I could not help but feel that they were the cause of all the trouble.

I remember I had my troop of guns down in the Jordan Valley, just outside Jericho, and with me was a great friend, Archie Wilder, who commanded a platoon of the Black Watch. We thought it would be great fun to shoot duck from the Allenby bridge which spanned the Jordan Valley. I therefore placed my guns upriver from the bridge and fired a creeping barrage up the river, which drove the duck over the bridge where Archie and I were standing.

This was highly successful, except that I put a round into the Emir of Jordan's summer camp on the Western Bank. This drew an immediate complaint from him and I was hauled up in front of the Commander-in-Chief of Palestine. We then returned to Cairo and rejoined the Regiment, in order to start training for desert warfare.

The Regiment was now training for desert warfare. In Egypt at that time we had a cavalry brigade and an infantry brigade, together with artillery and ancillary arms. Most of them had only recently been mechanised. We were operating as an armoured division under the command of General Hobart, who was a well-known armoured corps officer. He kept us hard at it and when Italy entered the war nine months later we had very little track mileage left and so were restricted in movement until replacements arrived. The Commander-in-Chief in the Middle East was General Archie Wavell, who was a very remarkable man – taciturn and reserved. I had known him when he was commander of the 2nd Division in Aldershot, before I went to Ireland.

Interestingly, the Wavells had a daughter, Joan, who was about my age and in 1935 I used to be asked to escort her to Deb dances. First of all there was dinner at the Divisional Commander's residence and then Lady Wavell, known as 'Queenie', Joan and I would motor up to London in the Divisional Commander's limousine. Lady Wavell, a stickler for etiquette, always insisted on sitting between her daughter and me! General Wavell was a classical scholar and a great student of poetry. He could recite endless poems from memory and produced an anthology of poetry in 1943 entitled *Other Men's Flowers*. The final poem in this anthology is one which he himself had written entitled Sonnet to the Madonna of the Cherries. I quote it:

> Dear Lady of the Cherries, cool serene,
> Untroubled by our follies, strife and fears,
> Clad in soft reds and blues and mantle green,
> Your memory has been with me all these years.
> Long years of battle, bitterness and waste,
> Dry years of sun and dust and eastern skies.
> Hard years of ceaseless struggle, endless haste,
> Fighting 'gainst greed for power and hate and lies.
> Your red gold hair, your slowly smiling face
> For pride in your dear son, your King of Kings,
> Fruits of the kindly earth and truth and grace
> Colour and light and all warm, lovely things.
> Through all that loveliness, that warmth, that light
> Blessed Madonna, I go back to fight.

This was written when he had been recalled from the Middle East in 1941 and when he thought he was going to return. Instead he was made Viceroy of India. Wavell never got on with Churchill, largely because he could not converse and make his case against Churchill's endless arguments. He had responsibility for Egypt, Eritrea, Sudan and Syria, with very few troops, most of which were unmechanised. However, he managed to hold the Ring until 1942, when reinforcements arrived. He had an ADC called Sandy Reid-Scott, who had lost his right eye. Wavell had lost his left eye. On their way back in 1941 they made a forced landing in Gibraltar harbour and had to swim to shore. They had with them a number of red boxes and were seen swimming in concentric circles, trying to recover them.

At Abbasia, in addition to the 3rd Regiment RHA, we had

the 8th Hussars, the 7th Hussars and, a little further out, the 11th Hussars, in all of which I had many friends. In the evenings we would probably dine in one or other of the officers' messes and then descend on Cairo for the evening's entertainment. The main hotels were Shepheard's and the Mena House, both of which were worth visiting. Later in the evening we visited the nightclubs in the rather more sordid parts of the city. The Egyptians were delighted to see us as they relied on our activities for their livelihood. At night the wide pavements of Kasr el Nil were dotted with tables at which the locals sat and drank coffee and smoked their hookas. A favourite game would be to drive our cars down the pavements doing a 'bending race' around the tables. I don't wonder that the Egyptians got rid of us from the Delta after the war!

I had many friends amongst the young married officers living in flats on Gazireh Island. Amongst them was Peter Hobbs, a Gunner, who married Sylvia in Cairo Cathedral in 1940 and whose son was my godson. Tragically, Peter Hobbs was killed in the desert in 1942. Another couple was the Hore-Ruthvens; Pat Hore-Ruthven married Pamela Fletcher, whom I had known before the war, and I saw much of them. Their son, Grey, was born in 1939 and is now Lord Gowrie. Pat, sadly, was killed in a raid behind enemy lines in the desert in 1942, when he was with the SAS. Another friend with whom I spent many amusing evenings was Hermione, Countess Ranfurly. Her husband was in the Sherwood Rangers and was taken prisoner in the desert whilst I was in Tobruk. His wife defied every regulation, remaining in Cairo and becoming secretary to the Head of Special Operations.

Whilst in Cairo I had several days' very good duck

shooting. Miles Lampson, the High Commissioner, used to be allotted a certain number of guns and usually invited a few army officers who were on leave. It took place about thirty miles from Cairo in the Delta and there were about twelve to fifteen guns. We started shooting at 6 a.m. and finished by about 11 a.m., having normally shot about a thousand duck. The guns did not have dogs and the birds were retrieved by small boys, about three to a gun, who swam round retrieving the birds.

King Farouk always had to have the best position and the largest bag – he probably shot about three hundred. This was probably due to the fact that he had two Egyptians standing behind him who shot at the same time as he did. Miles Lampson had the next best stand and was a good shot. Simon Elwes, the famous portrait painter, was a great friend of mine. He was a 4th Hussar and was a liaison officer at HQ in the 1st Armoured Division. I knew him well and saw a lot of him and, in fact, have some of his sketches. One day he was sent for by Miles Lampson to paint a portrait of Queen Farida. After he had been away for about three weeks we heard he had suddenly been sent back to the UK for having made a pass at Farida. Whether it was successful or not I don't know, but knowing Simon Elwes I suspect it was!

CHAPTER 5

The War Continues

WAR STARTED WITH ITALY late in 1940, when the Italians crossed the border between Libya and Egypt in the area of Salumn and advanced to Sidi Bahrani. We moved out in the desert and concentrated around Mersa Matruh, where we sat for some time facing each other. We formed columns of mixed arms, armoured cars, infantry and our 18 pounder guns and chivvied the Italians in their camps in the desert. In one of these forages we captured an Italian general, General Manzoli (a somewhat stereotypical Italian officer) in his staff car, in which he had not only two charming Italian ladies but also the latest records, one of which, I remember, was 'Run Rabbit Run'. We captured this but not the ladies! However, this came to an end when we pursued the Italians from Badia right back to Bengazi and were brought to a halt by the withdrawal of the troops, who were being sent to Greece.

This was a fascinating period and probably the most enjoyable part of the war. Perfect weather – warm days and cool nights. The desert held a tremendous fascination for me – absolute silence, no pollution and wonderful flowers near the coast. We lived and fought in small units, each based on the troop or platoon formation, living on our vehicles with officers and soldiers sharing the same food and suffering the lack of water – we had less than one gallon per day per man. Maps were inaccurate and we were dependent

The Desert Campaign 1941.

upon a compass, either sun or magnetic, to determine our position. If we were not accurate the supply echelon would fail to find us to deliver the rations each night. After dark we formed a close leaguer – all vehicles close together and camouflaged so that they could not be spotted by any aircraft in the moonlight and before first light you broke leaguer and dispersed so as not to provide a target from the air. In the summer it was not dark until 11 p.m. and the first light was probably about half past three, so the nights were short and sleep was restricted.

With me in the desert was my driver, Gunner Raine. He had been my driver since I returned from leave in 1939 and stayed with me the whole of the war until I returned to England in 1944. He drove my vehicle, looked after me and when I was at Staff College in Haifa acted as my batman and became a very close friend. Though he was meant to be my driver he really was a menace behind the wheel and was nicknamed 'Wrecker Raine' by his colleagues! He did show a great regard for my dog Helen and was a much better dog handler than he was a driver. Nevertheless, Gunner Raine was a wonderful chap and I was very lucky to spend so much time with him during this difficult period. He was from Newcastle and had been training to be a jockey before he joined the army. Though I wanted to keep him with me for as long as possible we were separated when I was sent to America after the war.

My Dalmatian dog, Helen, I brought out when I came back from leave. She was with me throughout the Desert Campaign and Italy and I brought her back to England with me in 1944. It was not very usual to have a dog in these circumstances but she was very dear to me and had been a gift from Maureen Stanley who bred Dalmatians. No-one

Italian prisoners at Sidi Barrani.

minded her being there and she was loved by most of the men. Even General Creagh would beg for her to stay with him when I went out on enemy raids. She was for a time in kennels in Cairo, where I had to leave her for about six months. During this time, King Farouk, who also had Dalmatians, used her to have a litter by one of his dogs – without my permission, I may say! Helen played a central part in my life for five years of the war and was perfectly described by my mother, who wrote the following account of her life for *The Field* in 1956:

Helen

This is the story of Helen, a very beautiful Dalmatian, perfectly marked with black spots. She had a great sense of humour and when anything amused her, or she had done anything especially wicked, she smiled a broad smile, showing all her teeth.

When war was imminent in 1939 she went to Egypt with her master (Brian Wyldbore-Smith) a Gunner, to join a RHA Regiment and here begins a story of great devotion and faithfulness – spoilt and pampered in England by us all, we knew she would be happier with her master even if she had to join in the fighting of the Italian and the Hun. For the first year she lived in comfort in Cairo, sharing her master's room and never leaving him. A terrible snob, she would have nothing to do with any Arab or Egyptian.

One day she was left guarding B's clothes on the shores of the Mediterranean while he bathed, and one of the troops was sent down to him with a message, but unluckily the man went too near his clothes and was bitten by Helen, which necessitated both the soldier and Helen being taken to hospital to be inoculated and tested against hydrophobia. Luckily all was well. The man soon recovered and beyond

Gunner Raine, my driver/batman.

having hysterics when she saw the needle, Helen was set free with a chit to say she had only 'misbehaved herself in a fit of excess of zeal'.

She was shown about that time at a special Dog Show in Cairo, where the King of Egypt was showing several Dalmatians who were supposed to be unbeatable, and with great pride Helen carried off the silver cup, which wasn't exactly popular in Royal circles. Unluckily, her cup was lost during the next years of war.

When the Italian campaign began Helen never left her master and, although usually of a timid nature, joined with the troops, never getting in the way and never leaving the guns. If the firing was very heavy she would dig a hole in the sand by the side of the guns and go down, just peeping out occasionally to see if her master was still there and all right.

Right across N. Africa she went with the troops. Hungry – she never worried, but caught desert lizards and ate them. Frightened – she only shivered, and tired – she never gave in. Only once she nearly lost her life in a terrible sandstorm which swept the desert for two days. Every man had to live in a gas mask and a mask could not be fixed on Helen. Her master's batman saved her life by letting her lie on a camp bed and holding damp cloths over her nose and mouth for all the hours while the storm lasted, but Helen rose up cheerful as ever.

On over the Desert she went with the tanks and guns and armoured cars, never getting in the way – cheering the men with her funny ways and being a wonderful companion to her master.

Mersa Matruh, Sidi Barrani, Derna, Bengazi, she knew them all. Then came the retreat when the Italian army had been finished off by General Wavell – but we had to send men to Crete so had to retreat. When it was necessary to shut her up in the desert because of the pie dogs, the troops

Helen in the desert.

made her a cage of wood with iron bars in front, and there sat Helen miserably with the name of her home painted above, 'Virtue Villa'.

So back and back our army was driven till they nearly reached Alexandria. Then came Alamein and on to Tunis and at Alamein no dog was allowed with the troops, so Helen was put into kennels at Cairo again as on the morning of the great barrage at Alamein an order was given that every dog was to be shot, for fear they should bark and give movements away.

After Tunis was taken and the Hun finally expelled from N. Africa, Helen's master was sent for seven days' leave to Cairo, where he flew with General Horrocks and when the seven days were up B. hadn't the heart to send her back to kennels, so off she went with him to start another campaign. It was difficult to take her as they were to fly and no dogs were allowed in aeroplanes, but Helen started off gaily with one of the Generals' names on her collar.

Then came a time when B. was given a battery and they had a few months of rest in Tripoli. During that time Helen blotted her copybook and had three puppies, which made all sorts of difficulties. She was not a good mother and her one idea every evening was to bury the puppies in the sand and jump round B. till he found them and dug them out. Before the puppies were a fortnight old the RHA battery he was commanding was ordered to Italy and no dogs were supposed to be taken, but Helen was hidden in an armoured car with the three puppies in a box. So the first of the world they saw when they opened their eyes was the Bay of Salerno.

The other day I had an article in the Royal Armoured Corps Journal shown to me. It was called 'Tanks in the Vineyard' and was an account of operations of the 1st Royal Tank Regiment near Naples in October 1943. The words I found were:

'Helen was the code word and the 69th M— Regt were
to fire concentrations at "H" hour on the first objective . . .
On receipt of the code word "Helen" (the origin of which
was the name of Major Wyldbore-Smith's Dalmatian bitch)
the troops were to move etc.'

and as that Helen has been my constant companion for the
last six years since the war, and has just been put to sleep at
the age of fourteen-and-a-half years, I am trying to tell her
story while my tears are still not dried on her grave.

Dorothy Wyldbore-Smith

Mother of the Gunner in this story, who owned
this Dalmatian and who is now a Major General.

Three weeks after we arrived at Bengazi, the Germans
landed a force in Africa. This was commanded by General
Rommel and he had with him a Panzer division and 90
Light Division. Within a very short time he had mastered
the desert warfare and attacked our very small number of
troops in the Bengazi area and driven us back to the border
with Libya and Egypt. It was at this time that General Wavell
was replaced, first of all by General Auchinleck, who was an
Indian Army officer and never really understood desert
warfare. I myself became adjutant to a very famous man,
General Jock Campbell, who later on in the war earned a
VC at Sidi Resegh for leading a charge in an open car against
a mass of German tanks. During that period we used to take
columns of guns and infantry and attack the enemy by going
around its flank in the desert.

The Italians were terrified of the desert and stuck to the
coast road. They formed forty-five camps in which they
stayed, except for occasional patrols. Jock Campbell formed
mobile columns of troops consisting of a company of

infantry, anti-tank guns, artillery and armoured cars. We attacked these camps having moved through the night. One such operation took place when we had Colonel 'Strafer' Gott with us. He and Jock Campbell were old friends and they and their wives used to hunt with the Belvoir Hounds. As we watched the Italians running in panic and firing wildly in every direction, 'Strafer' Gott turned to Jock Campbell and said, 'Just like a good five mile point. Wouldn't our wives love it.'

Jock Campbell was a very good friend of mind and had been a horse gunner who was very fond of playing polo. He was outgoing, attractive and extremely popular in society. Though he was an amateur soldier, as were many of us at this time, he became a Brigadier. Sadly, he was killed when he was being driven along a coast road. The vehicle ran off the road and into a sand dune. Jock Campbell broke his neck and was killed. I always feel that this was a terrible and wasteful death and remember him with fondness.

In October 1941 I left the Royal Horse Artillery to go to the Staff College in Haifa, on a course which lasted four months. This was the last thing I wanted to do and I regret to say that whilst there I did not really distinguish myself. My reluctance to go to the Staff College was due to the fact that I was having such a good time working with Jock Campbell who used to write letters detailing exactly what I was missing. My friends and I, all fellow students who had all been fighting in the desert, thought little of instructors who had no battle experience. I remember one night we found them all correcting our papers in the instructors' study and we locked the doors and turned the hoses on them so they were swimming around with all our exam papers. This was not considered a good thing!

Before the end of the course, a naval cousin of mine, Hugh Wyldbore-Smith, who was serving in the cruiser *Ajax*, arrived in Haifa and asked me to dine in the wardroom that night and watch them conduct a shoot against the Free French in Syria, about seventy miles north of Haifa. I accepted with pleasure. (Incidentally, my cousin was killed when he was serving on the *Hood* which sank, drowning the two thousand men on board.) After a number of pink gins we moved off up the coast and I watched a most entertaining bombardment by *Ajax* against the French positions. As we were about to return to Haifa in the early hours of the morning, the Admiralty ordered *Ajax* to proceed at full speed to Malta to defend a convoy. Obviously this had not been my intention but as I was not able to jump ship I sat back and enjoyed the experience. Thirty-six hours later we arrived in Malta. There was nothing I could do so I was put ashore there and got a lift back by air to Palestine, arriving back at Haifa Staff College, having been absent for four days.

This was the final straw. The Commandant, General Dorman-Smith, failed to see the joke and despatched me as a staff captain to Tobruk. This was meant to be a punishment but in fact, Tobruk, which was then besieged, was a wonderful experience. The only way to get in was by submarine as the harbour was totally surrounded by enemy ships. It was my first time in a submarine and I was quite intrigued by the experience. The journey took about seven hours and was probably one of the most unusual trips I have ever made. When I arrived I was attached to the 9th Australian Division, a magnificent body of men. For six months we withstood the attacks of the German army, until we were eventually relieved.

I then joined the 1st Armoured Division as Brigade Major to Brigadier Fowler, who was the Commander, Royal Artillery. During the next two months we were driven back by Rommel to within thirty miles of Alexandria. What follows is history. Montgomery arrived from England and took the place of the existing Field Commander.

Since the breakout of the 70th Division from Tobruk we had suffered a number of defeats by Rommel's forces in the fighting around Sidi Resegh. In the first battle of Sidi Resegh, my ex commanding officer, Jock Campbell, now commanding the 7th Armoured Divisional Support Group, earned his VC. In the same battle, a subaltern of mine named Gunn, in the 3rd Regt RHA, earned a posthumous VC. Although imposing heavy casualties on the Axis forces, we were eventually driven back to the Alamein position. It is generally said that our tanks were inferior to the Germans'. Certainly they had a few which were superior, i.e. the Mark IV and the Tiger, but we had a large superiority in numbers. The main reason for our failure was the fact that they had the 88 mm anti aircraft gun, which they also used as an anti tank gun, with devastating effect. Furthermore, our commanding general, General Cunningham, did not understand the handling of armour and failed to concentrate his forces. Whilst Rommel led from the front, Cunningham ran the battle from the Divisional HQ well back.

With Montgomery's taking over of the 8th Army and General Cunningham being replaced, the desert war ceased to be a game. Furthermore, large reinforcements of ammunition, tanks and vehicles had arrived in the Delta. Montgomery immediately established a tactical HQ separate from the main HQ of the 8th Army, from which he operated until the end of the war at Lüneberg Heath. He made a number of visits to the troops, which were informal, with all ranks gathered around his jeep. 'I want to impress on everyone that the bad times are now over. There will be no doubters in the party and no bellyaching and no more withdrawals.' The effect was electric! No longer did we look over our shoulders with a view to withdrawing from Egypt but we looked forward to a chance to beat the Axis forces.

Though he was only a short, slight man (5ft 7ins and 147 pounds), far from being classically attractive and possessing a beak shaped nose, General Montgomery was hard to forget. He had piercing blue eyes which hinted at a ready wit and remarkable intellect and was a marvellous orator, frequently assembling his men around his staff car and boosting their flagging morale. He generally wore chukka boots, knee high socks, baggy khaki shorts and a khaki shirt with rolled up sleeves, topped by a black beret with two badges on it. This could be seen to reflect his preference for informal military dress and his aversion to anything like bureaucracy.

He was certainly a most talented military commander and he himself had a great and unflinching belief in his own talents. It was as though he thought that he could not possibly fail in any of his campaigns. This positive attitude was infectious and, whilst under his command, we rarely doubted our chances of success.

In recent years he has become one of the most contro-versial figures of the Second World War and is much maligned and misunderstood. He had fought in the first war to shake the world and had been badly wounded. When he recovered from his injuries he focused upon his career and had become a general by the beginning of the next war. When he was appointed Supreme Commander of the Allied Expeditionary Force he automatically became a direct subordinate of General Eisenhower. Additionally, he had control of all infantry manoeuvres in the Normandy campaign.

He wanted to avoid loss of life as much as possible and planned all his campaigns very carefully, believing that war was won or lost with the human life. I feel that many have been a little harsh upon him when criticising him for this caution and this regard for his soldiers made him the great man he was. General Bradley and RAF Bomber Command Harris in particular thought that Montgomery's interest in preserving the British infantry made him dependent on other facets of the military. More recently, however, those who have examined Montgomery's life and career have taken into account the difficult position in which he found himself. The fact that he had a great concern for his men has now earned him respect rather than criticism.

When I first became involved with Montgomery I was Brigade Major to the CRA of the 1st Armoured Division, Friz Fowler, and we were part of 13 Corps. It was to our HQ that the responsibility of the fire plan for Alamein was given. For a fortnight we worked on this plan for over a thousand field and medium guns. At 2300 hours on 23 October the Battle of Alamein started, with 30 Corps in the north and 13 Corps in the south. For seven days it hung in the balance but by 5 November we had penetrated their minefield and by 6 November the Axis Forces in North Africa had sustained a crushing defeat. Four German divisions and eight Italian divisions were destroyed and 30,000 prisoners of war taken.

We had been chased up and down the desert for some time until Monty arrived and put a stop to it. It was he who instigated the huge attack which transpired to be very

German prisoners at Tobruk.

successful. Even so, at the time it was very difficult to work out what was happening and whether we were making any real headway. The first four days of the battle were bad – we made little progress and suffered many casualties. However, when Monty decided to move our position and attack from the south our fortunes improved. This was my first major battle and quite an event in which to be involved. I was so busy ensuring that the fire plan was carried out correctly that I had little time to worry about my own fate, which was probably a very good thing.

After Alamein I was posted as Staff Officer to General Horrocks, who had taken over command of 10 Corps from General Lumsden, whom Montgomery had sacked for failing to act sufficiently boldly after Alamein. General Horrocks was another commander who led from the front. Gassed in the First World War, he had an implacable hatred of the Germans. He operated from a tactical headquarters, like Montgomery, and I, as his staff officer, used to travel in a tank with him. My job was to keep him in touch by wireless with Montgomery at tactical HQ and the leading elements of 10 Corps. We had a Grant tank and he used to sit in the turret watching the battle, while I was down by his feet manning the wireless set, unable to see anything of what was going on. He had great charm and I got to know him very well. In fact it was he who gave me my nickname of 'Rogue Elephant Jones', which stuck with me until the end of the war.

10 Corps had the job of leading the advance against the retreating Axis forces. The first major hold-up we met was at the Mareth Line, west of Tripoli. 13 Corps was left holding the front, while 10 Corps did a left hook and outflanked the Axis position in a very successful night

advance of twenty miles. During this period I frequently visited Montgomery's tactical HQ, as he liked to be situated close to his leading corps commander. The tactical HQ had a remarkable family atmosphere. Its members consisted of his military secretary Kit Dawnay, his ADC Johnny Henderson, a 12th Lancer officer whom I had known for some time, and a number of liaison officers whose job it was to keep him in touch daily with the situation on the front.

Amongst these was one Noel Chavasse, another, John Poston, an 11th Hussar and Trumble Warren, a Canadian officer. All of them were with Montgomery throughout the war. The atmosphere was extremely informal and very friendly and Monty treated them like a family, calling them all by their Christian names. They had a betting book, in which bets were recorded, some serious, and some frivolous. I remember betting Noel that my Dalmatian had more than sixty spots on her! Equally, I remember someone betting Monty that the war would not be over by the end of 1945. All bets were not only recorded but were also fully paid up and noted to that effect.

After the Battle of Alamein and before embarking for Tripoli I went back for four days' leave in Cairo with General Horrocks in his aeroplane. He knew that I had my dog in a kennels in Cairo and suggested I bring her to the desert with me when we went back. So I collected Helen from the kennels and we flew up in his 'plane and landed close to 10 Corps HQ. My driver/batman, Gunner Raine, took charge of Helen and I kept her with me until I returned to England in 1944. She had, naturally, an intense dislike of being bombed, almost as much as I did, and it was a close run thing as to who got into the slit trench first, Helen, Gunner Raine, or myself!

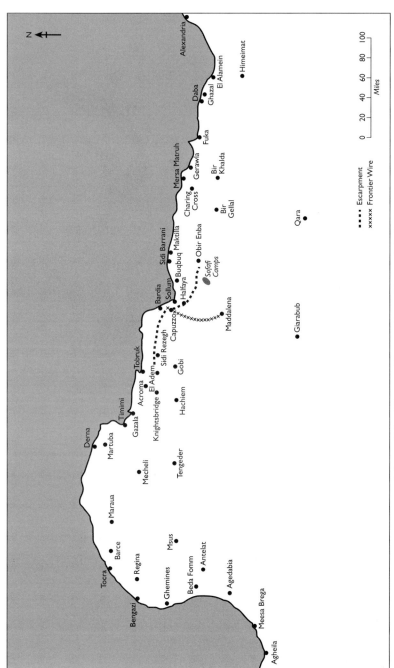

Map of the Desert Campaign: East of Agheila.

55

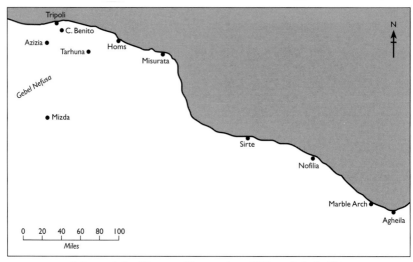

Map of the Desert Campaign: West of Agheila.

At about the same time as the battle of the Mareth Line, 'Operation Torch', which was the code name given to the landing by the Anglo-American force in North Africa, took place. After a time they were held up and it was decided by General Alexander to send General Horrocks over to command 9 Corps in the First Army there and to take with him the 7th Armoured Division and the 4th Indian Division from the 8th Army. Accordingly, we flew round and met General Alexander. We also had the 26th Armoured Brigade, a part of the 1st Army, under command and Brigadier Pip Roberts, with whom I was to be closely associated for the rest of the war, commanded them. Pip was a professional soldier and a great friend to me. He was a nice though slightly reserved man who did not participate in the social scene as much as someone like Jock Campbell but was still an interesting and appealing individual. It only took a matter of two or three days for the enemy to collapse and within a week all resistance in North Africa had ceased.

Chapter 6

Journey Towards Peace

AFTER TUNIS, MONTGOMERY, who always took an interest in my postings, thought it would be a good thing for me to have some regimental experience and I was posted as a battery commander to the 5th Regiment Royal Horse Artillery. I joined them outside Tripoli and for two months we did very little other than bathe and go into Tripoli. Having flogged up and down in the desert for more than two years we did not feel it necessary to do very much training. We thought we were going to be employed in the invasion of Sicily, but this was not to be and eventually, two months after joining, we took part in the landings at Salerno. My battery joined the 1st Royal Tank Regiment, which was then commanded by Colonel Michael Carver, in the 22nd Armoured Brigade, which was part of the 7th Armoured Division.

Having done some training with a landing craft in Tripoli, we arrived at the beaches, our guns got ashore with very little difficulty and we dug in on the beach. The only excitement was that an Arab dog had covered my dog, Helen, two months previously and she gave birth to three magnificent puppies right in the middle of the landing! This kept my driver, Raine, very busy but there were no problems and we all – dog, driver and myself – landed safely.

Having broken out of the bridgehead after five days, we bypassed Naples and crossed the Volterno and about twelve days later came to the next river, the Garigliano. The 1st Tank Regiment was detailed to lead the crossing and I provided the covering fire. First of all I managed to find an observation post up a church steeple but unfortunately was spotted and got shot out of it. I then climbed a telegraph post on the edge of the river, so as to observe my covering fire for the 1st Royal Tanks. Then an 88-mm spotted me and managed to hit me in the head and the elbow. The 88 is a very fast weapon and has great momentum. Indeed, I was actually hit before I even heard the bang. Luckily, I was strapped to the pole which prevented a nasty fall and was helped down by the wireless operator and managed to get back to Headquarters. I was in no way seriously wounded but it looked as if I might lose the use of my arm for a time.

I was evacuated to Naples and put on board a hospital ship bound for Bizerta, where a general hospital had just arrived from Chicago, with 300 nurses, 100 doctors and 600 beds. They were desperately keen to get into business and as the first patient I was subjected to every form of test and medical activity! I was fascinated by the hospital ship but it was not a very pleasant experience. I occupied the bottom bunk and I remember being covered in blood when the chap above me began to haemorrhage in the night.

After about a week I was much improved and the hospital was beginning to fill up. My ward became full of Americans and we were told that General Patton was going to tour the hospital the next day and present Purple Hearts to all the patients. I was not particularly anxious to receive a Purple Heart because most of the American patients in my ward were cases of venereal disease and so I somehow managed to get hold of my clothes and escape. The hospital was on the edge of a landing field and there I discovered a

Lysander, with a British pilot who had come over to get some drink for his unit in Italy. I asked him for a lift back and he agreed.

Unfortunately we landed on the wrong side of Italy at Bali and I then had to hitch another lift across to Naples where my regiment was. On arriving at Naples airfield, I was amazed to find Gunner Raine and Helen sitting in my truck on the edge of the airfield, where they had been waiting for me for the last ten days. Whilst I had been away in hospital, the division had been withdrawn from the line and were resting in Positano, on the Sorrento peninsula. I joined them there and had a wonderful month, doing nothing! We were welcomed by a Madam Galligurchi who was as pleased to see us as she had been to see the Germans a short while before. There were lots of young ladies who amused us – we ate, we drank, we saw places of outstanding natural beauty and a good time was had by all.

During this period, General Bobby Erskine, who commanded the 7th Armoured Division, paid me a visit and presented me with the DSO, awarded for the operation on the Garigliano, when I was wounded.

We then embarked on a troopship from Naples and set sail for England. I was very excited about going back to England as I had been away from everything that was familiar to me for so long. Gunner Raine and Helen, who had the run of the ship and got away with anything, were as excited to be going back as I was. I shall never forget steaming up the Clyde on 4 January at about 6 o'clock on a dark and misty night, standing with Raine and Helen on deck and getting the first sight I had had of England in four and a half years. On arrival, Helen was removed to a quarantine kennels and I went off on leave to join my mother at Berkswell, near Coventry, where she and my father had moved five years before. She had provided shelter in her home to a flood of refugees from Coventry. Added to this, she had received a telegram from the War Office saying that I had been wounded, so my arrival home did much to restore her health and happiness.

Unfortunately, she had suffered much in my absence and had recently found herself to be a widow. August 1939 was the last time I saw my father. My leave had ended and I was to depart for Egypt once again. He had been for quite some time very ill with asthma which had plagued him all his life and he died in 1943. I did not hear this dreadful news until two months after he had passed away and, though I was obviously grieved by his death, my lengthy absence had somehow cushioned the blow.

Additionally, my father's death did not come as a surprise. He had been very ill for a great period of time and my mother had selflessly nursed him for years. His death came at a very turbulent time and had a profound effect upon my mother. The family had moved from Thorpes Thewles to another parish near Coventry. My father passed away very soon after the infamous bombing of Coventry city and my mother, being seen as the head of the parish, was besieged by parishioners who had been made homeless by the terrible air raids. This bombing undoubtedly hastened my father's death and put a great strain on all those close to him. My mother showed immense courage and valour and tended both to my father and to those who petitioned her for help.

As if all this was not enough, my mother was told that I had been wounded in action and this too proved to be a strain upon her. Though war is harsh and difficult for those who are on foreign shores fighting the enemy, it is also cruel to the loved ones who wait anxiously at home, wondering if and when they will see their men again.

My brother was a great help to the family at this time as he was nearer than I, working in munitions in Scotland. Nevertheless, I think that my mother was very relieved when I returned home from Egypt on leave and felt glad that she had not lost two family members in such a short period of time.

CHAPTER 7

The Aftermath of War

ON 10TH JUNE HQ 11th Armoured Division embarked at Portsmouth on an LST and, twenty-four hours later, disembarked near Bayeux. We set up our HQ about three miles inland. During the next three days the remainder of the division arrived. General Roberts and I visited Montgomery at his tactical HQ nearby and also General Connor, who commanded the 8th Corps. It was not until 21 June that we were told about our first operation, which was to force a crossing over the River Odon, about six miles west of Caen.

During the next six days we made slight progress and the division settled down to fight under its new commanders. Unfortunately the commander of the 159 Brigade proved inadequate and was removed by Pip Roberts and replaced by Brigadier Churcher, who remained with the division throughout the rest of the war. 29th Armoured Brigade was commanded by Brigadier Roscoe Harvey, a dashing 10th Hussar. Both of these two Brigadiers were excellent but very critical of each other and my job as GSO1 was to act as mediator and prevent them having a direct confrontation. It was essential that we got the best from these two capable Brigadiers and maintained the smooth running of the Regiment. Because they had to talk to each other indirectly through me a great many arguments were avoided.

Each day, just before first light, the general would leave

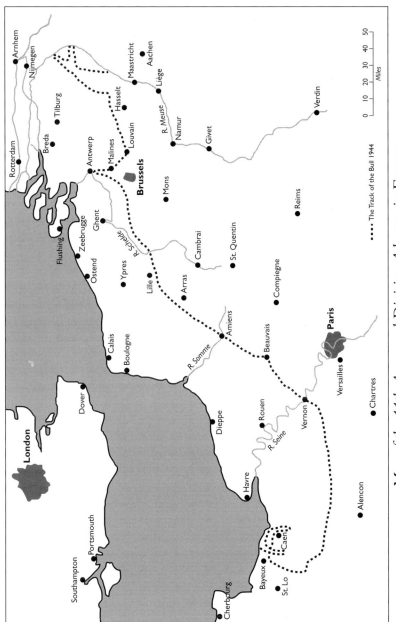

Map of the 11th Armoured Division Advance in Europe.

63

divisional HQ with his tactical HQ consisting of his GSO2 and his ADC and move up to the leading units. I would remain with divisional HQ in my ACV with two GSO3s, wireless communication to tactical HQ 159 Brigade 29th Armoured Brigade and a rear link to Corps.

During the next three weeks we were involved in several other operations, none of which achieved the desired break-out. However, on 18 July we took part in Operation Goodwood, which was an attack by the 7th, 11th and Guards Armoured Divisions to break out west of Caen. The 11th Armoured Division led and at 0045 hours on the 18th the heavy bombers of Bomber Command, followed by the 9th US Airforce, came over with the best part of a thousand planes and dropped a carpet of bombs. Heavy fighting followed for the next three days, during which time we lost 734 men and 200 tanks and advanced about 16 miles. Divisional HQ was bombed on the second night and I had two out of my three ACVs knocked out. On 20 July the operation was called off and we withdrew into reserve.

Although we failed to break out we inflicted very heavy losses on the enemy and drew onto our flank the seven Panzer divisions and four heavy tank battalions, which allowed the Americans to break out on the other flank very shortly afterwards. Montgomery always said that he never really thought we would break out at Goodwood but the impression he gave at his briefing before the battle was quite clear in my mind. Nevertheless, the result was that the operation played a vital role in the final break-out by the Americans.

After Goodwood, the Division was withdrawn into reserve, awaiting the breakout at Falaise. On 31 July we were on our way, advancing on the left flank of the Americans,

ACV Team, 11th Armoured Division.

through Le Beny Bocage to the River Souleavre. On 3 August, after six days of continuous fighting, we were counter-attacked by 10 Panzer Division, reinforced by Tiger tanks from the 2nd Panzer Corps. The battle raged all night, with heavy casualties on both sides, and in the morning the enemy withdrew. On 12 August, we came under the command of 30 Corps, which was then commanded by General Horrocks, who had returned after being wounded in an air raid in Bizerta.

There now followed a period alternating between exhilaration and frustration. Some days we advanced up to fifteen miles and other days were held up for several hours by mines and determined resistance from small parties of German tanks. However, on 27 August we reached the Seine and crossed it with little opposition. Our blood was now up and we were advancing approximately twenty miles a day on two centre lines, our sights fixed on the River Somme and Amiens, about sixty miles ahead. We replenished about 1600 hrs and then continued our advance by night, with a full moon.

In order to keep direction we shone searchlights on the centre line to act as a guide. The troops were quite exhausted and at some stops drivers went to sleep and had to be woken up. Frequently we found odd German vehicles had joined our column. At 0500 hrs our leading troops reached the outskirts of Amiens and I found our main divisional HQ alongside a German field bakery, which was accompanied by a Mark 4 tank. This we destroyed before relieving the field bakery of its load!

At this stage we were under the impression that we were heading for Brussels and Brigadier 'Roscoe' Harvey, who commanded the 29th Armoured Brigade, told the 23rd

Hussars that the next day they were to liberate Brussels. This news raised our spirits even higher than they already were. However, on 1 September we heard that the plan was changed and that the Guards Armoured Division was to go for Brussels and the 11th Armoured Division for Antwerp. On the afternoon of 4 September, our leading troops entered the town of Antwerp to scenes of wild rejoicing. There was very little resistance in the town itself, which was fortunate, as all the tanks were festooned with excited inhabitants clambering over them and offering wine, bunches of flowers and kisses to the crews.

We were held up by a bridge being demolished over the main canal and although we cleared some of the dock area, we failed to clear it all. It was, in fact, the biggest port in Europe.

The 53rd Division now took over from us on 12 September and we reverted to being under the command of 8th Corps. This was at the time when Montgomery was having a major row with Eisenhower over the supply problem. All supplies were still coming from the beach head in Normandy, some 1200 miles away, General Bradley was trying to break into the Ruhr with his army group and Montgomery was trying to advance on the left flank with his. Eisenhower insisted on advancing on a broad front, with both sides receiving the limited petrol supply, rather than a concentrated effort by 21 Army Group.

As illustrated by this example, it is clear that Monty and Eisenhower did not get along at all well with one another. The problem was that they were so very different. Eisenhower was a brilliant politician and statesman, a good diplomat who had to relate well to all the nations under his command. He had not a brilliant military mind like Monty who could plan and execute battle strategies so well but who lacked some diplomatic tact. They had different roles which they both carried out to the best of their considerable abilities. Monty can be seen to have had a rather limited view. He wanted all the supplies to himself and, though I was totally loyal to him and regarded him as a close personal friend, I could understand how other people found him difficult to work with.

At this time Montgomery thought I was due for some Regimental experience and I was posted to the 179 Field Regiment (Worcestershire Yeomanry), which was an artillery regiment in the 43rd Wessex Division. It was a great wrench to leave the 11th Armoured Division, and, above all, General Roberts, with whom I had been associated not only in the desert but all the way through Europe.

Our advance from the Seine was probably one of the most successful armoured operations of the war. During this period Chester Wilmot, the Australian War Correspondent, was representing the BBC and attached himself to our main HQ. He sat in my ACV and listened to all the wireless links, observing the workings of the Division. He was a very nice man and I got on well with him. At night, when Pip Roberts came back with his tactical HQ and joined us at Main HQ, Chester Wilmot would join with him and me at Tac HQ mess and we would discuss the day and play liar dice. Chester was not much good at this and generally lost! He wrote an excellent account of this period in his book, *Struggle for Europe*, just before he was killed in an air crash in 1954, long after the war had ended. It was interesting that my wife, who knew Chester Wilmot was with me at my HQ, could tell exactly what I was doing by listening to his nightly despatches on the BBC news.

On 10 September 'Market Garden' took place, in which 101 Airborne Division was dropped to secure the bridges at Nijmegen. Most of the Army Group artillery was in support and 179 Field Regiment fired thousands of shells in a fire plan greater than that of Alamein. For my part, I had little to do and I found it frustrating to have such an inactive role after the previous four months with 11th Armoured Division.

Shortly after my arrival in the Regiment, Montgomery sent for me and told me I was to write a pamphlet called 'The Armoured Division in Battle', based on the methods used by 11th Armoured Division in its advance from the Normandy bridgehead to Antwerp. I spent a fortnight at Tac HQ, 8th Army and lived in one of his personal caravans. This was much more comfortable than the surroundings I had been used to and I enjoyed this short break immensely.

While I was there the Ardennes offensive by two Panzer armies took place and rent a hole 50 miles wide on the flank and rear of 21 Army Group. I had almost finished my pamphlet. Montgomery would return in the evenings full of cheer, having been put in temporary command of Hodges' 1st Army and Simpson's 9th US Army. He would tell us of an evening what had happened in battle that day and was quite vivacious and lively, especially for a man upon whom so much responsibility had been placed. A month earlier he had been made a Field Marshal, King George having invested him on a visit to his HQ. At this time, James Gunn, the artist, was staying at Tactical HQ, painting the Field Marshal's portrait. Also living there at that time was Kit Dawnay, a young military secretary, Johnny Henderson, Monty's ADC who was very young and had just been called up when he left school and Noel Chevasse, another young

Montgomery on Rommel.

officer. He was sent out by Monty every day to discover what was happening on the front line and this enabled Monty to get an extremely accurate picture of the situation, which was not always possible. In the evenings, after Montgomery had examined my efforts with the pamphlet and rewritten part of it, we would spend a very relaxing time in the usual family atmosphere.

Just before Christmas I returned to my regiment, which was then deployed in the Reichswald, supporting 43rd Division in its advance to the Rhine. It was bitterly cold weather and snow lay fairly deep. There was some quite heavy fighting for about ten days, until we crossed the Rhine and headed into the Hanoverian Plain.

After crossing the Rhine I was given two companies of infantry and ordered to clear the area of Hamburg Zoo. This we did with little opposition, the main concern being to ensure that the animals had enough feed. From here we made our way down towards a village called Melandorf, about twenty miles from Hanover, and whilst we were here the Armistice was declared, on 5 May 1945. For several weeks we stayed in great comfort on farms, collecting a considerable number of souvenirs. I acquired a Mercedes touring car, two horses and a very attractive stray dog. In order to keep the troops employed, I organised a hunter trials, which was great success, with a large number of entries from all units in the Hanoverian Plain.

I had quite a lot of contact with the German people at this time and I found that the Bürgermeister of the local town was very helpful towards us. In this part of the countryside there was little damage and we encountered no major problems. The people did not display any animosity or ill feeling and seemed as relieved as we were that the war was finally over. They were also very grateful that we were helping stabilise the situation in Germany. The clearing up operation was good and very effective, something I was pleased to be involved in.

However, I did not have much compassion for the Germans after the war and felt much the same way about them as I did about the IRA in later years. Later, of course, I did change my view towards them but at this time, when the events of the war were still very fresh in my memory, it was not so easy to be compassionate.

In July, when demobilisation had already started and I think we had got rid of our guns, I was told to organise a camp for about 20,000 displaced persons – mostly Ukrainians and East Germans. When I returned home I took with me a Ukrainian couple from this camp. They became my cook and my gardener and were a delightful couple who were with me for about six years, until they emigrated to Canada. We heard years later that the husband was involved in setting up a chain of hotels. The Ukrainians were a very nice couple and I was delighted that it turned out so well for them.

Though obviously very relieved that there was to be no more fighting and unnecessary loss of life, I felt somewhat let down at the end of the war. It seemed to be something of an anticlimax for me and I could not recall what life had been like before the advent of war. I had become so used to fighting and having a strong and secure purpose in life that I was quite at a loss about what to do next. I felt that I should perhaps leave the army and embark upon another career though the prospect did not fill me with a great deal of relish.

My close friend Pip Roberts left the military when the

war had ended and went to work for a famous biscuit company in London. He persuaded me that this was a wise career move and encouraged me to apply for a job in this same firm. This I did and attended an interview with the Managing Director of the company. Perhaps fortunately, I took an instant dislike to this individual who took an equal dislike to me and I did not get the job. This was largely due to the fact that I had independent means, something of which the character in question did not approve. It later transpired that Pip Roberts was not treated very well by the firm as he was fired after a while and I was quite glad that I had not been successful in my application. It was to be some time before I left the army and I was to have many interesting experiences before I embarked upon my next career.

CHAPTER 8

Married Life

UPON RETURNING to England one leave I renewed my acquaintance with Molly Cayzer who was later to become my wife, the younger daughter of Lord Rotherwick, who was head of the shipping firm Clan Line and later Union Castle. During the previous years I had met her a number of times on the debutante circuit and had been included in some of the dinner parties before the deb dances. I knew both her mother and her father. Her mother was a most wonderful woman, Penelope Rotherwick, known as Freda. Her father was a brilliant businessman and always most charming to me. She had an older sister called Pamela and two brothers, one of whom sadly contracted polio during the war and was plagued by this for the rest of his life. The other brother eventually became Lord Rotherwick and carried on the family heritage. They lived in a lovely house called Tylney Hall in Hampshire, with many thousand acres and a wonderful garden. This was certainly a very comfortable home and visually very pleasing.

While I had been away overseas fighting in the war, my future wife had been by no means idle in regard to the war effort. She enlisted as a WAAF, something which was very unusual and unlikely considering her privileged background. She had a fairly responsible position and was in charge of overseeing the balloon sites. Consequently, she was not at home very much and contributed a great deal to her position which she took seriously. Molly, despite having all the advantages of wealth and class, was not a spoiled or precocious young woman. Indeed, her parents lavished most of their attention on her male siblings and Molly grew up level headed and well grounded.

I remember a very unfortunate incident dating from my earliest associations with Molly. While I was on leave in 1939, Molly came to stay with my family at Coleshill, where my father now had a parish. This was a much bigger parish than Thorpe Thewles and he was much better paid – £1500 a year as opposed to £700! Such was their excitement at this increase in their finances that they engaged a butler by the name of Milner. He joined Anne Langthorne, our daily, who had been with us for fifteen years. Unfortunately, Milner, unbeknown to my mother got rather too close to Ann and put her in the family way and she had a miscarriage. That was the end of Milner!

I do believe that I fell in love with Molly immediately and it certainly was a case of love at first sight, on my part at least. I found her to be a charming and captivating young lady. Not only was she physically very beautiful but she possessed a strong mind, something which had been lacking in my previous romantic interests. I vividly recall seeing her at a dance at 21 Knightsbridge. She was coming out of the ladies' powder room and I was struck by her brilliant twinkling eyes, sunny smile and lovely complexion. Upon speaking to her I realised that Molly was by no means just a pretty face and she held well considered opinions. I found her tremendously interesting and felt that here was a perfect combination of beauty, charm and intelligence.

Though I had not been considering marriage before meeting Molly, as life was too uncertain because of the war, I instinctively knew that she was the woman with whom I was destined to spend the rest of my life. This feeling proved to be correct and we have enjoyed a long and very happy marriage.

I asked her to meet me in London for a party two weeks hence and at the end of January we met and went dancing together. That evening I became engaged to her. In those days I could not afford to waste time! At any moment the Second Front might open up in France and I never knew when I might be off again! Molly was staying at the Mayfair hotel and my mother was her chaperone. Mother was very tired this particular evening and specifically requested that Molly did not wake her when she came in. However, in the excitement of becoming engaged, Molly had left her handbag, containing money, identity cards and all the necessities of life, in the taxi and upon realising this immediately woke my mother to ask her what to do. Luckily, the taxi driver brought it back.

I went down to Tylney Hall to ask permission of her father for the engagement and I remember arriving at the Hall, which was a most comfortable and delightful house, and going into the garden with Lord Rotherwick to help him prune the rhododendrons. In the library, which looked onto the garden, were Molly's mother, her aunt, Lady Jellicoe, and her sister, Pamela Hamilton-Russell. They were busy thumbing through Debrett's *Peerage* to see who this extraordinary young man was whom Molly had produced. I think they were slightly relieved to find that I did appear in it under the name of Smith Marriott and had a pedigree which went back a few hundred years. I was made very welcome and we announced the engagement forthwith. We aimed to be married at the beginning of April but nothing could be certain in those days, as by then I might well have been sent to France.

There was no engagement party as is often favoured nowadays as it was at this time enough of a difficulty to organise the wedding itself, let alone the other frivolous trappings of matrimony. Additionally, this was during the time of rationing and with the wedding so close an engagement celebration was deemed unnecessary. We were engaged, married and honeymooned in one month – quite a whirlwind romance.

Meanwhile I had been posted to the 11th Armoured Division as GSO1 to the new general, Pip Roberts. It was Montgomery's plan before the invasion that experienced commanders and staff officers from North Africa should be posted to brand new formations and units which had been training in England. Many of the soldiers in units back from the desert were battle weary and knew where it hurt but the new formations were highly trained and eager to fight. This was therefore a most successful plan. For example, General Roberts had fought for three years in the desert and commanded a division. Friz Fowler was the CRA, I was the GI and four of the commanding officers came from units which had fought in the desert.

The marriage was welcomed by both families and this made things much easier than they might have been. The match was considered to be a good one and was approved all round. My wartime wedding was in stark contrast to the lavish affairs of today and, because of the tumult and uncertainty of this period, we only had a week to plan the wedding and honeymoon. This proved to be something of a blessing as I was much too busy and preoccupied even to begin to feel nervous at my impending nuptials, though I

Wedding, 1 April 1944, Savoy Chapel.

was very excited. Amusingly, we were married on 1 April but the wedding itself, which took place at the Savoy chapel, was a very pleasant affair. The ceremony and reception were very simple but no less enjoyable because of this simplicity. Most of the guests were in uniform and there was a distinctly wartime flavour to proceedings. Our reception was held at 21 Knightsbridge, where Molly and I had fallen in love, and was thoroughly enjoyable. I must confess that I am unable to remember much about the reception or the wedding presents as there was so much going on. Both myself and Molly, who had been a WAAF, were concerned about the events in Europe and the war loomed large in our minds.

I was not the first of my friends to embark upon married life and had many married friends in the military. Although we were engaged and married in the space of a very short time, Molly and I were not too young when we fell in love. I was thirty and she twenty-seven; both of us had lived and experienced a great deal and both knew the serious nature of the commitment we were about to make.

General Roberts said I could have a week for a honeymoon, unless he had to recall me should the landing take place before the middle of April. So off we went to Great Fosters hotel in Egham, where we spent a wonderful week honeymooning. We had a very splendid room in the hotel and the time we spent together was most enjoyable. The grounds and gardens too were quite something and were filled with beautiful flowers. Most of our time was spent in and around the hotel as I did not have a car at this time and could not travel anywhere. We had arrived at our honeymoon destination by train along with half the wedding guests who were travelling in the same direction. After our brief foray into wedded bliss had come to an end I rejoined the division, which had moved from Yorkshire to Aldershot in preparation for embarkation. I managed to move my wife into a hotel in Aldershot, where I was able to spend the nights.

Then, towards the end of May, we were ordered into the embarkation area, which was, of course, sealed off. I could tell no one, not even my wife. I could only ask her to go back to her parents and to pack my clothes, which my batman would fetch. At that time she only knew what was happening by the flights of bombers and transport aircraft crossing the sky on the night of 5 June, and the arrival of my batman to collect my clothes. Although we did not know it, she was already pregnant. To leave the comfort and security such as she had had for the past twenty-seven years, with all the uncertainty of war and a husband whom she hardly knew and would not see again for more than a year, and after her child was born, must have taken great courage.

It was to be quite some time before Molly and I could enjoy a normal family life. I was in France and Germany until the armistice and then travelled to Washington to learn about military training. Indeed, for eighteen months we were never together as a family for more than four weeks at a time. I feel that the marriage was invigorated by the early birth of a child who added a new effervescence to our marriage. Our early married years were dogged by lengthy absences and much uncertainty but we weathered these storms somehow and went on to share many great experiences together. During the next twenty-two years, we lived in twelve different houses, varying from a beach hut on the Bitter Lake to Constable's Tower at Dover Castle. She made each one into a home for a minimum of two dogs and, eventually, five children.

On 11 December my daughter Carolyn was born a month early in the middle of a shooting party at Tylney Hall; there was no time for Molly to get hospital. Consequently, Carolyn was delivered on the dining room table – quite a traumatic way to enter the world. I had previously arranged with Johnny Henderson that a message would be sent through to Tac HQ 8th Army and he was to let me know, no matter where I might be. On 12 December I therefore duly received the message from Johnny that I had a daughter and that she and her mother were doing well. It was therefore with great surprise that on 2 January I received an official signal from the War Office to the effect that my wife had given birth to a daughter. I thought at first that it must have been a delayed twin rather than a delay in the official notification! Although I may have at first wanted a son, as many fathers do, I was absolutely delighted when my daughter was born and the prospect of fatherhood filled me with excitement and anticipation.

We were eventually able to set up our first home which was an attic in Putney with three bedrooms, a living room, a minute kitchen and a bathroom. It was whilst we were here that my second daughter, Angela, was born on a very cold night in February. It was snowing hard and I had only just managed to get my wife to the Middlesex hospital in time. That winter was one of the coldest in history and we lived in greatcoats huddled in front of a gas fire, which frequently went out through lack of gas! However, after the privations of war it was heaven and we had some wonderful respites staying with my in-laws at Tylney Hall and at Lanfine, a lovely house in Ayrshire with a very good grouse moor. It was about this time that my father-in-law bought up all the liberty ships at the end of the war for a very small price and then took over the Union Castle Line – a brilliant piece of business.

Over the years Molly gave birth to five children, four girls and then a boy. Five children would obviously be a great deal of work for any mother, especially when coupled with an absentee father, but Molly was aided by engaging a wonderful nanny. She was a charming woman called Miss Bully and the children became very fond of her. We had advertised for a nanny and she responded to our advertisement. At first, she was not keen to take the position as she had wanted to work abroad but when it became clear that I would be working abroad a great deal she decided to come to us. This transpired to be a fortuitous decision for both parties. Miss Bully would often stay in England and look after the children whilst Molly made fleeting visits abroad to be with me. Our nanny quickly became an integral part of family life and stayed with us for twenty years, being a nanny to the younger children and a companion to the girls when they got older. She died in 1964, very suddenly at Charing Cross Station just after visiting our family in Dover.

Before the children were sent away to school they were taught at home by Molly who operated under the PNEU system which she found to be very effective. It did seem to give the children a head start and provided a good grounding in education.

Our children were brought up in accordance with the customs of the time and there are many differences between the methods employed then and those favoured now. My children became very independent owing to the schools they attended and the fact that they were not cosseted by either Molly or myself. They also had the opportunity to travel a great deal and sampled the delights of Germany, Singapore and the Middle East at a very young age. They were encouraged to be confident and made a host of friends in many different parts of the world.

As they grew up they began to establish their characters and all traversed a different life path. Carolyn, my eldest daughter, had a desire to act and completed a course at the prestigious English drama school, RADA. It was here that she met a Canadian actor who was later to become her husband. For a time, the two acted together in theatre plays and Carolyn displayed great promise. However, her acting career was cut short when she married and had children. Her husband continued to act, somewhat unsuccessfully, whilst she stayed at home and raised two daughters, Melissa and Lucy, and a son, Sam. Sadly, Carolyn's marriage ended after twenty-five years and she was left to provide a stable family life alone.

Her younger sister Angela was of a slightly more domestic bent. She ran a clothes shop for a time with Penelope, my third daughter, but was to give this up when she met her husband who was an accountant. The couple settled in Wiltshire and have two daughters, Jemima and Emily, and a son, James.

Penelope was possibly the most worldly of the children and had ambitions. She gained a degree from York University before enjoying her coming out season at Dover Castle. She later married James, the son of Pat Herdman whom I had known all those years ago while stationed at Northern Ireland, and moved to the picturesque scenery of Ireland with which I had been so struck as a young man. Together they ran a linen business and have a son, Emerson, and a daughter, Katie.

My youngest daughter, Nicola, was to lead something of a

tragic life. For twenty years she was a normal, happy and healthy young girl and participated in the same activities and attended the same school as her elder sisters. She liked sport and hunting and was successful at both. However, at the young age of twenty she developed schizophrenia, a debilitating condition which plagued her for the rest of her unhappy life. Her illness, which could only be controlled with heavy medication, meant that she was constantly being admitted to clinics and care homes – something which she hated. Nicola had problems dealing with her terrible condition and, failing to cope with the hand she had been dealt, found solace in drugs. This was to lead to her untimely death in 1996 when, under the influence of drugs, she fell from a window and was killed. Though this was a tremendously upsetting and traumatic event, Nicola's siblings and their children saw first-hand the disastrous results of drug use which was to prevent them from experimenting with substances themselves.

My son Robin was born in 1957 and attended St Ronan's school before becoming a pupil at Eton. Though I feel that Eton is a marvellous school for those committed to taking full advantage of the opportunities it offers, it transpired to be a poor choice for Robin. He was not very self-motivated and needed encouragement which was not provided at Eton. However, he did enjoy rowing and was in the second eight at Eton. King's School, Grantham, of which I was a governor, is a much better school for boys like Robin and the pupils are given much encouragement. This kind of grammar school would have suited him much better. Robin did not want to go to university and instead set up home in a house we owned in London. He went into business for himself making railings and security shutters and later

Bournehill House.

branched out, supplying pool tables for pubs. He married
late in life, at forty-two, and has been quite successful.

We lived in a great variety of homes over the years, some
of which stand out in my memory far more than others.
Bournehill was one such family home. We lived here for a
period of sixteen years beginning in the 1950s and really
enjoyed this time. It was a wonderful base for the family and
boasted 180 acres of farmland and a Friesian dairy herd.
Originally, the house only had 50 acres of land but we
purchased the land from two neighbouring farms and
developed both the gardens and the farmland. The Friesians
did not make much money but helped reduce our tax bill
greatly. We sold Bournehill in the 1960s and the next owners
split the land up into smaller packages and made a
substantial profit on it.

Because of my military responsibilities the family was

posted to a great variety of different locations in a fairly short space of time. We lived in a great many places, some of which were lovely, some not so good, but all added to our experiences as a family. As one might expect, we soon became accustomed to moving house and regarded it as an ordinary way of life. We lived for a time in a lovely old German house in the river Weser in 1957 and I have happy memories of this dwelling also. Similarly, our Suez Canal home in Egypt was very charming and was provided by Molly's father, who sat on the Suez Canal board. Unfortunately, it was about twenty miles from the regiment and so I spent a good deal of time travelling. Dover Castle too was incredibly good living and we occupied Constable's Tower which had excellent views. Here we had a very good staff and it was a wonderful place to entertain guests. Other houses were not so pleasant, particularly the service houses, and none of us were very taken with the home we occupied in Aldershot. This was a military house and the army quarters were, generally, very bad. They were poor dwellings which had been built very cheaply and had no real character to speak of and the houses which were in the local areas were always of a much higher quality.

Though my family means a great deal to me I played a very different role in family life to that assumed by fathers today. The fact that Molly and I married during the war years and the nature of my profession at this time meant that I was not always on hand, either as a father or as a husband. Though this may seem odd to the younger, modern reader, it was simply accepted as a matter of course during this period of social history. Even after the war had finally drawn to a close I was away from home a great deal, serving for several years in Malaya and the Far East. This resulted in our

Celebrating the author's 80th birthday with family.

living a married life which was completely different to that experienced by young married couples today.

Our marriage was a partnership in which Molly played a significantly larger role than I and took on responsibilities of home and family without complaint. This has had a great effect upon establishing the very close relationship which we have now. Yet all these early difficulties cannot have had too detrimental an effect upon the solidity of our marriage and, despite these lengthy separations, Molly and I are still together and very happy today.

CHAPTER 9

Post War Employment

AFTER THE WAR had drawn to a close I thought that I was
eventually to go home to be with my wife and child.
This was not to be and in August I was posted to the British
Military Staff in Washington in order to study the role of
American training methods. I was told that my wife and
daughter would be able to join me in about four months.
After a fortnight's leave, during which I was able to see my
daughter for the first time and also visit my mother, I
departed for the US leaving my family living in a cottage
near Tylney. I set sail on the *Queen Mary*, which was packed
with American soldiers being repatriated.

Within two months of my arrival the atomic bomb was
dropped in Japan and the war came to an end. However, it
took the War Office some time to reorganise my posting, so
I set myself up in a flat in Washington and concentrated on
the local race meetings, managing to attend on twenty
consecutive days. During the course of my study of
American training methods, I managed to visit Chicago (a
military butchery), Fort Dill, Texas (School of Infantry),
Fort Leavenworth (the armoured warfare establishment),
Los Angeles (the army photographic school) and the Rockies
(the army winter warfare school). It was a wonderful way to
see America, with all expenses paid. I must confess that, after
the war, I considered this American posting to be something
of a holiday and took every opportunity of enjoying myself. I

certainly concentrated more upon the social aspects of life in
the States rather than centring on my job. Despite this, I did
discover that, on the whole, the American training methods
were far superior to those employed in Britain.

The only sad thing about my time in America was that I
was not allowed to bring out my family after all. Molly's
parents were a tremendous help to the family at this time
and she occupied a house at Bournehill, which was only
three miles from their own residence. This was a comfort to
both Molly and myself. She found solace in the fact that,
though her husband was overseas, her parents were always
on hand and I was relieved that they were so close which
made me less inclined to worry for her.

Later my wife became very involved in my working life
and it was easier to combine the two distinct elements of my
life – career and family. Molly got on very well with people
from a great variety of cultures and backgrounds and was
eager to get involved in the military and, much later, politics.

In December, I received instructions to return to the UK
to become Military Assistant to the CIGS. It was a great
boon to get this job and it was a stark and pleasant contrast
to the nomadic life I had been living for so many years. At
last I was able to settle with my family and relished the
prospect of commuting to Whitehall each day rather than
labouring through the desert and never knowing what each
new day was going to bring.

Field Marshal Montgomery had now taken over from
Field Marshal Alanbrooke and organised his office within
the War Office rather on the lines of a Tac HQ. Staff
consisted of Lt Col George Cole, the Senior Military
Assistant, myself, a major, a GSO3, and Johnny Henderson,
the ADC. Between us we had to look after the CIGS and the

Vice CIGS, General Simpson, produce all their papers for meetings and briefings, and make all the arrangements for travelling. I looked after General Simpson for the most part but also Field Marshal Montgomery when George Cole was otherwise engaged. The major concerns at this time were re-employment of the army, settling Germany once again and the increasing problems in India and Palestine, with which Monty in particular was very concerned.

Field Marshal Montgomery, having been a brilliant army group commander, was not so successful as the Chief of the Imperial General Staff. Unable to work with the other Chiefs of Staff, the weekly meetings were a continual battleground. Air Marshal Tedder, Chief of the Air Staff, was his *bête noire*. In those days Montgomery was living in a flat at 7 Westminster Gardens and at Christmas the Chiefs of Staff used to give each other signed photographs of themselves instead of Christmas cards. Tedder's photo was hung in the lavatory and when I went round to Monty's flat with some papers after a stormy Chiefs of Staff meeting I would find Tedder's photo with its face to the wall!

I worked with Montgomery for some considerable time and came to know him very well. People have often asked me whether or not the great General was a nice man and the answer would have to be a resounding 'No'. Indeed, no-one who was in Montgomery's position, who had seen the things that he had seen, who had to bear his responsibilities and make such weighty decisions, *could* be a nice man. He had many excellent qualities – he was kind, he was fair, he was strict and he had a tremendous drive and energy but 'nice' he was not. Montgomery seemed to get on better with the younger officers and was very relaxed with the young members of staff in the War Office. With older officers he was tense and more reserved and perhaps became a little unpopular with them because of this.

This job was not an unpleasant one and involved quite a large amount of foreign travel. I journeyed to India where I bought a car, a Standard, which I sent to England. Just after the war cars were not readily available in Britain and I was in a privileged position being able to buy one abroad. We discussed partition as a solution to the problems the country was experiencing but little decisive action was taken. I was only in India for a very short time and do not remember very much about the country. Additionally, I did not see a great deal as I spent most of my time in a very large and comfortable hotel rather than travelling round this very different environment. I also travelled to Canada in a work related capacity and had a meeting with the Vice Chief in Montreal before journeying north. Again, I was very busy during this brief trip and did not see much of the country.

Whilst working for Montgomery, I enjoyed some wonderful holidays. One that really stands out in my mind was a skiing holiday in Austria. At this time, you were only permitted to take £25 out of the country at any one time and, even in those days, this was not a considerable sum. Nevertheless, Molly and I spent a very pleasant fortnight skiing in the Austrian mountains, lodging at a private girls' school in the region. The teachers at the school were excellent skiers and really put us to shame but this did not prevent us from having a thoroughly enjoyable time. We would also escape from the stresses of working life by holidaying in Molly's parents' home in Scotland.

CHAPTER 10

More Military Responsibilities

IN 1947 I WAS POSTED to the Staff College at Camberley, as a member of the directing staff, with the local rank of Lieutenant Colonel. I was in C Division, which was established at Aldershot and Molly, three daughters and one Labrador moved to an army quarter in Steeles Road. Penelope, my third daughter, was born during the move. Whilst as a house it was an improvement on the flat in Putney, it was in a row of officers' quarters in an unattractive part of Aldershot garrison. I enjoyed my time at Camberley as I was able to live a more focused and secure kind of life. I was also delighted that I was allowed to live a normal family life and thrived on the constant company of my wife and daughters. It was quite a relief not having to snatch a week here and there and to become more of a presence in my burgeoning family.

I was placed in charge of sixty students and had to teach military history, most of which was concerned with the World War I had just fought in, tactics, man management and the usual military curriculum. There was an emphasis on practical facets of the army as well as lectures given by prominent military figures. This was a post I held for eighteen months and, I must confess, I regarded it as something of a holiday after fighting in the war for so long.

Whilst at Camberley I was told first of all that I was to go as military attaché to Abyssinia and was then told that I was going to a coastal defence regiment in Singapore. Having spent most of my service in the Royal Horse Artillery, I was appalled at the prospect. Much of the war had been spent operating with the Royal Armoured Corps and I had many friends in Cavalry regiments. One in particular, Desmond Fitzpatrick, to whose son I am godfather, asked me if I would go as second-in-command to his regiment, the Royal Dragoons, with the prospect of commanding them in about four years' time.

Desmond Fitzpatrick was very much an up-and-coming soldier. He was already a Brigadier and was to finish his service as a full general and Gold Stick. However, it was a big step for me to leave the Royal Artillery after sixteen years' service and join another corps. Other Gunners had done it but not always successfully. I wrote to Field Marshal Alanbrooke, who was then Master Gunner, telling him of my dilemma and asking his advice. He wrote back a most charming letter in which he said that he thought it a very good thing for the armoured corps to get the benefit of the experience of an officer who had had a not unsuccessful war as a Gunner and advised me to transfer.

The die was cast and I joined the Royals at Wolfenbuttel in Rhine Army, very close to the border with Russian occupied territory. It did not take long for me to become adjusted to my new role and we moved from Aldershot to a very nice German house in a forest near Wolfenbuttel. It was a well built house with some land and had previously been used as an officer's house. This was near the Russian controlled zone and part of my role here involved ensuring that no-one crossed this border. By this time our household consisted of three children, one nanny, one Labrador and one cocker spaniel and life in Germany was very pleasant.

I made many friends and acquaintances during my period in Germany and got to know people quite well. The officers were a charming group of people and many had their families out there. We all quickly became great friends. Ten miles away was the town of Brunswick, which had an excellent nightclub to which Molly and I paid frequent visits, in the company of other members of the officers' mess.

The regiment moved to Egypt in 1949. I was not particularly enamoured about this move but had little choice in the matter and had to accept it as a necessary part of military life. The main reason for my reluctance was the fact that there were no married quarters in our new camp and, after having become used to family life, I was rather loathe to leave it behind, albeit for a short time only. They were situated at Fayid, on the Bitter Lake, halfway between Suez and Ismailia, living on a tented camp with very few facilities. I went ahead with the dogs and Molly returned to England with the children. I travelled to Egypt on a boat and had to share a cabin with a very fat Turkish gentleman. He had the bottom bunk whilst I had the top. Unbeknown to him, my Labrador had accompanied me on the journey and slept under his bed. It used to get up during the night and prowl about, causing him to believe that our cabin was haunted!

At that time my father-in-law had moved from Tylney Hall to Sedgwick Park in Sussex and we bought a house about two miles away near Horsham with about 200 acres of farmland and some cottages. This was to be a base in England for the family when they could not accompany me abroad. After three months Molly came out to Egypt to join me.

Luckily Molly was invited to come out to Egypt by the Commanding Officer but we had no official quarters and lived for a time with the commanding officer of the regiment, Roddy Heathcoat-Amory, and his wife Sonia. At first we camped in their dining room and then in a beach hut on the shores of the Bitter Lake which, though primitive, was better than living in a dining room! Fortunately, Lord Rotherwick was a director of the Suez Canal at that time and through him we managed to get a house in Ismailia which belonged to the Suez Canal Company. This was a very comfortable house located about twenty miles from the Regiment and there we remained for about nine months. I then managed to get a flat in a house near Fayid, to which we brought the children and nanny.

During this time we managed to pay a few visits to Cairo and Alexandria, sometimes to play in polo tournaments, and once when we stayed with the Peels in Alexandria. Teddy Peel was a cotton magnate and he and his wife Nora had been very kind to me when I was in hospital with jaundice in 1941 and had me to stay for a fortnight to convalesce when I left hospital. At this time relations with the Egyptians were strained and we evacuated the Canal Zone in 1951, the Royals then returning to England.

At the end of the year I was promoted to Lieutenant Colonel and went as GSO1 to the 7th Armoured Division in Germany. Soon after this posting Molly returned to England and gave birth to our fourth daughter, Nicola, after which she rejoined me in Germany. It was a great joy to return to the Division with which I had spent so much of the war. The Divisional HQ was at Verden, about thirty miles from Hanover, and an attractive market town. The Divisional Commander was General 'Splosh' Jones, who was an energetic and delightful commander. We worked hard and I was able to organise the HQ on much the same lines as the HQ of 11th Armoured Division in the war.

One evening, after a dinner party at our house in Verden, at which General Jones and his wife were present, my GSO2, a young officer, his wife and I all set out for a nightclub in Bremen. About halfway there my GSO2, who was driving his car, with Molly and me in the back, hit a bridge over the River Weser and we were left suspended. All of us except Molly were temporarily knocked out and an ambulance arrived to take us to hospital. Fortunately Molly arranged for us to be taken back to Verden and prevented a blood test being done on the driver! None of us was severely injured, but the German police started an investigation as to whether drink had played a part in the accident. General Jones, who insisted that when he left dinner we were all as sober as judges, saved the situation!

In 1953 our armoured car regiment was the 15th/19th Hussars, which was due to move to Malaya as a result of the state of emergency which had been declared following the murder of the governor. Just before they left the Command-ing Officer, Lt Col Butler, was removed and I was offered the posting in his place. I was delighted at this posting, as I knew many of the officers from the desert campaign and also knew many of the regimental families, who came from Durham and Northumberland. It had always been a 'family' regiment, with a number of sons and fathers serving. I joined them at Wesendorf and had three weeks to get to know them before flying out with an advance party to Singapore, leaving Molly, once again, with the children, nanny and dogs at home in Bournehill House. The regiment followed by troopship a month later and we were put up in Selarang Barracks just outside Singapore, before moving north to Ipoh.

On my first visit to Singapore I found it to be very civilised, comfortable and appealing but it was not until later when I became Chief of Staff there that I got to know the country well. We had to cover the whole of the northern border with Thailand and prevent terrorists infiltrating from across the border and attacking the local population. It was an unusual role for an armoured car regiment and much of our work was done on foot, with the regiment split up into very small parties. I do recall throwing some splendid parties in Ipoh and these helped to raise the morale of the regiment immensely. After they had been patrolling in the jungle for several weeks, they liked nothing better than to return to the base and enjoy some fairly wild gatherings. These served to revitalise them and renew their vigour.

As Commanding Officer, there was little I could do except to go around encouraging the men in the various areas of the jungle in which they were operating. It was one of the happiest periods of my career and I had a magnificent regiment to command. It was the days of national service and I am always fascinated to think of the many men who joined us for just two years and then went on to great success in civilian life. Ian Gow was one who joined us for national service. When he left us he went into Parliament and became Margaret Thatcher's PPS until he was tragically blown up by the IRA in 1988.

Molly, three children, nanny and two dogs now joined me in Ipoh and we lived in a very comfortable Malayan type house, with open verandas and blinds all the way round. It was right on the edge of the jungle and I remember one day

The house at Ipoh.

Molly discovering a cobra just outside the front door. She managed to dispatch it swiftly with a golf club!

The climate and was warm and humid but there was a hill station at the Cameron Highlands about twenty miles away which we used to visit and where it was always delightfully cool. At one time I had a small hut up there and we used to go up with the children and my batman. It was deep in the jungle and one weekend whilst Molly was there with the children some tiger cubs were sighted at the back of the hut and we discovered the next day that there was a tiger's lair only about a hundred yards away.

When not working we played polo and bathed in the sea, which was wonderful. I managed to collect about a dozen polo ponies and most of the officers of the regiment learned to play. We ran a very happy regiment and it was always a tradition that relationships between officers and troops were close and of the very best. We enjoyed ourselves greatly, sometimes to excess!

I remember that after a very convivial guest night I took all the officers down to the local swimming club, where we dived in, some of us still in our mess kits, and had a tremendous party. This, unfortunately, upset the local inhabitants, who thought we were not treating their club with sufficient respect. I had to go and make an abject apology the next day to the club chairman and we were all barred from using the club for the next six months, even though the wives (and my nanny) were still able to go on using it. I therefore used to get Nanny to sign me in.

The area in which the regiment was deployed consisted largely of rubber plantations and the planters were very hospitable. The only trouble was that if you went out to lunch with them on a Saturday you would be extremely lucky if you arrived back home by Sunday evening! During the two-and-a-half years we were there we had few casualties – only about ten people killed. We worked extremely hard and it was quite a strain patrolling in the jungle in that climate, never knowing when you might be ambushed. The troops used to go out on patrol for a month at a time and then return to Ipoh to recuperate. Back at Ipoh the officers played polo and there was excellent bathing in the sea. I collected something like twelve polo ponies and any officer who wished to was able to learn to play the game.

The Malayan campaign was one of the last successful operations conducted by the Services until the Falklands. By the time I left in 1956 the terrorists were on the run and, in fact, one of the last jobs that the regiment did whilst under my command was to send a patrol up to the Thai border and pick up the leading terrorist, whose name was Chin Peng, from the jungle and bring him down for negotiations at army HQ.

It was with considerable sorrow that I gave up command of the Regiment and returned to the UK for a spell at the Staff College as an instructor at the end of 1956. Following our return Molly gave birth to a son whom we called Robin and we now decided to settle at Bournehill. Whilst at Camberley I was GSO1 of B Division, under the command of General Hewetson. I had a rather uneventful year and spent the weekdays living in the officers' mess, returning home for the weekends.

In 1957 I was sent to the Imperial Defence College, which was situated in Sleaford House in Belgrave Square. Lectures started at 9 a.m. and finished about 4 p.m. It was an interesting year and at the end we did a tour of Europe, the Far East, the Middle East, Africa or America. About fifteen of us, under the guidance of one of the directing staff, visited the heads of government and leading statesmen in these countries. I went to Africa, starting off in Kenya and proceeding to Swaziland, South Africa, Basutoland, Angola, Nigeria and Ghana, the final stop being Morocco. South Africa was still deeply involved in apartheid and Angola was still Portuguese and highly organised – very different from the situation there today. As with so many of the places I have visited, I have few clear memories of Africa owing to the fact that I travelled around so quickly and had so much work to do whilst I was there.

In Nigeria I stayed with a local Nigerian magistrate who had been educated at Oxford and was a delightful man. I attended his magistrates' court one morning, at which a local witch doctor was up in front of him. He was accused of failing to ensure a rainfall during the previous month and received a month in gaol. Afterwards I asked the magistrate if he really thought this a just sentence and he replied that if he had not sentenced the man it would have destroyed his reputation as a witch doctor. In Ghana I was invited to take part in a polo match. The local natives rode without stirrups and their bits were made of wire, but their ability to hit the ball was infinitely superior to mine.

At the end of the course I was posted to the War Office as a Brigadier in a new directorate called 'Combat Development'. It was an interesting job in which one was looking ahead to weapons of the future. The head of the branch was one John Mogg, later to become General Sir John Mogg. He was great fun, with a splendid sense of humour, and we travelled together to America and Canada to meet our corresponding numbers in the American and Canadian armies. Whilst in New York we managed to spend a night on the town, during which I lost my passport. John Mogg was most helpful in dealing with this situation.

All the time I was at the Imperial Defence College and the War Office from 1957 to 1962 I was able to live at Bournehill House. We started a farm and had a herd of about fifty Friesian cattle. I don't think we ever made much money but we covered a lot of expenses and lived quite cheaply. I was able to shoot in the winter as my father-in-law had a good shoot on his property next door to us.

In 1962 I was appointed Chief of Staff to the Far East Command. This was one of the first unified commands to be created by Lord Mountbatten, then Chief of the Defence Staff. By no means popular with the service chiefs, the Labour government, with the backing of the Chief of Defence Staff, had pushed it through. One afternoon,

General Sir Richard Hull, then Chief of the Imperial General Staff and head of the army, saw me and said that my appointment was Chief Staff Officer rather than Chief-of-Staff. This meant that I would only bear the rank of Brigadier, rather than that of Major General.

The next day I was sent for by Lord Mountbatten to be briefed on my job. He told me of the importance he attached to this as the first unified command covering the whole of the Far East, from Singapore to Hong Kong. This was a great challenge. At that time it was vastly unpopular with the three services; the last thing they wanted was a unified command as it cut into the powers and positions that each service commander had held before. I told the Chief of the Defence Staff that I understood my posting to be that of Chief Staff Officer and not Chief of Staff, according to General Hull. Whereupon Lord Mountbatten picked up the telephone and asked to speak to the CIGS. 'Hull,' he said, 'I hear from Brigadier Wyldbore-Smith that you have altered his posting to Chief Staff Officer. If you wish to remain CIGS you will correct this posting to that which I ordered.' By the time I got back to my office in Whitehall I had been reinstated!

When I arrived in Singapore the Army Commander, whom I knew well, sent for me. He said that he was delighted to see me out there but did not want me interfering in any way in the army's affairs. I received a similar message from the Air Force Commander and the only person who was sympathetic was the Naval Commander because the Commander in Chief was a senior officer in the navy. This was Admiral Sir David Luce, a most delightful sailor who gave me a great welcome.

It was fortunate that after I had been in Singapore for three weeks the revolt in Borneo blew up suddenly and one night there was a mutiny of native troops in Brunei. For a time it looked as if we were losing control there. The three service commanders were away in Hong Kong, either on holiday or at a conference, I cannot remember which, but I know that at 0100 hours I was summoned by the Commander in Chief, Admiral Luce, to the operations room. He said, 'Look, we've got this crisis on our hands and we cannot wait for the service commanders to return. We will have to take charge ourselves.' We therefore despatched battalions of infantry, ships and squadrons of aircraft to Borneo and by the time the service commanders arrived back two days later we had got the thing completely under control. This proved the efficiency of a unified command and how it cut through the delays inherent in the committee type of command which existed before.

Soon after my arrival in Singapore, Molly, five children, Nanny and two dogs joined me. I had been allocated a delightful quarter – a large old-fashioned eastern type house, with a large garden and tennis court, next to the High Commissioner's residence in Nassim Road. We had a good Chinese staff – a 'number one boy', two maids, a cook and a gardener. I also had an ADC, one Captain Burge, a Gunner. Next door to us in Nassim Road was the Residence of the High Commissioner for Malaya, Lord Selkirk. My house had a tennis court, which his did not. It was made out of red laterite clay, with a very short run-back and a ditch about six feet from the back line. Lord Selkirk used to enjoy playing singles with me and would come round in the evening for a game. Neither of us was a very good player and he frequently fell into the ditch at the end and walked home covered in red clay!

Whilst here I played polo at the Singapore Polo Club and,

House in Nassim Road, Singapore.

in fact, became its captain before I left. We travelled around playing matches against the teams of the Sultans of Pahang and Jahore in Kuala Lumpur and Penang. The polo was not high class but we had a lot of fun and it provided an amusing social life, both for me and for Molly.

The eldest three children were now at school in England but would join us in the holidays and we had a governess called Miss Colbert who was known as Coco, who looked after the younger two and gave them lessons. Coco was an excellent governess but was plagued dreadfully by Robin who used to bang on her window at night pretending to be a burglar. Whilst here, Molly went on a trip with the Commander-in-Chief, Sir David Luce, and his wife to Australia and had a wonderful time, seeing a lot of the country and its wildlife.

As Chief of Staff I travelled extensively to Hong Kong, Australia, Malaya, Borneo and Saigon and Molly was able to accompany me on many trips. We worked closely with the police force in Borneo and during much of this time I used to fly to Kuala Lumpur for meetings with the Police Commissioner each morning at 0700, arriving back in my office by 1100 hrs. After a year Admiral Luce returned to the UK to become Chief of the Naval Staff and was replaced by Admiral Varyl Begg, another delightful sailor with whom I got on very well and whose wife and family were friends of Molly. He ran a very efficient and light-hearted HQ and we saw a lot of him socially, at dinner parties and receptions.

Denis Healey was Defence Secretary at that time and visited us on several occasions. Lee Kwan Yu was the Prime Minister of Singapore and a very efficient politician. During the Profumo affair, when John Profumo was sacked from the Cabinet because of his affair with Christine Keeler, Lee Kwan Yu, who was dining with the Commander in Chief, said to me, 'I cannot understand you British. You sack a member of the Cabinet for having an affair, but I would be suspicious of anyone in my Cabinet who was not having one'! Of course, he was wrong insofar as Profumo was sacked for misleading the House of Commons and not for a sexual indiscretion. Algy Cluff, a member of the Guards Parachute Company, then seconded to the SAS, was in Singapore at that time and we used to play polo together at the Singapore polo club. He has been a friend of mine ever since.

Whilst in Singapore, Molly and I visited Angkor Wat, the ancient temple in Cambodia. We flew to Phnom Penn and then on to Siem Rep and spent four days exploring this fabulous area of temples in the jungle. Four hundred years

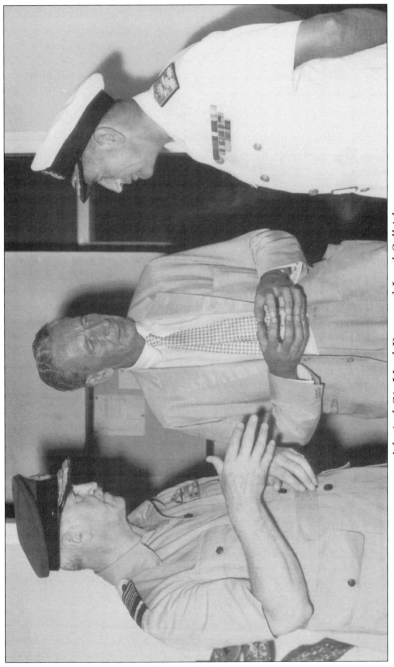

Admiral Sir Varyl Begg and Lord Selkirk.

old and much of it still overgrown by jungle, it covered sixty square miles and was populated by some local Cambodians, who acted as guides. Shortly after our visit the Cambodian civil war started and for the next ten years it was impossible to get there.

I also visited Saigon during the Vietnam War and stayed with the military attaché, Colonel Henry Lee, and his wife Peggy, a charming couple with whom I was closely associated during the fifteen years following my retirement from the army. He arranged for me to visit the Vietnam military academy at Dalat by helicopter. Molly came too and on the way back to Saigon the American pilot pointed out some Cambodian troops in the jungle north of Saigon. He then flew down low and, much to their surprise, sprayed the area with automatic fire. Molly enjoyed this trip enormously!

CHAPTER 11

Settling Down

IN 1965 I RETURNED to the UK for my final appointment before retiring. I was lucky enough to be made GOC the 54th Territorial Division based at Dover, with Territorial units in Kent, Sussex and London. I also became Deputy Constable of Dover Castle and had a residence in Constable's Tower within the Castle. The Castle itself has a remarkable history and is part of the fine heritage of Kent. It was from this tremendous vantage point that the Celts watched Julius Caesar's invasion in 54 BC and was also the site of the first Roman fort and lighthouse. After the legions had left Britain it was invaded by Angles, Jutes and Saxons and the Bishop Odo of Bayeux arrived in 1066 with a pre-fabricated castle.

The actual castle in which I was to live dates from 1200 and fended off an attack by the French in around 1216. By 1330 the castle had been strengthened by the introduction of cannons which had a range of three miles and during the Napoleonic wars caves were built inside to house the thousands of troops needed for the war against France. The changes made to the structure of the castle during this period included the huge curtain walls being reduced in size to accommodate heavy gun platforms and the extension of the underground tunnels. Later it was remodelled by Hubert de Burgh who introduced the secret passages, fortified gatehouses and sally ports. These measures made it

Constable's Tower, Dover.

much easier for the British military to attack enemy invaders. The castle had played a role during both World Wars too and was the Headquarters of the Dover Patrol in the first war whilst being used as a shelter during bombing raids in the second.

The grounds in which the castle stands boast many fine relics and buildings of historical importance. Remains of the Iron Age hill fort can still be seen as well as the Roman lighthouse which was used to guide Roman ships into port. The Saxon church of St Mary remains intact and the famous Constable's Gate can also be seen. The underground tunnels, used by Winston Churchill himself, are present too and the castle is the most complete building of its kind in Britain. I certainly felt very excited and privileged to be staying in such an esteemed historical location.

I was supplied with a considerable staff of a chef, two maids and a gardener. We lived in great style in this lovely old castle with a superb view across the Channel to France. The 15th/19th Hussars supplied me with an ADC, one Bunny Connolly-Carew, a delightful young officer with a wonderful sense of humour and enormous charm, which he used to great effect on all the inhabitants of Kent. He could be relied upon to organise dinner parties with thirteen guests! He had a delightful Dalmatian dog, a breed for which I have always had a very soft spot since the days with my own Dalmatian, Helen, in the desert. Bunny's Dalmatian had the unfortunate habit of relieving himself against the very magnificent curtains in the drawing room!

I remember being very impressed with Dover Castle and was happy to live there, knowing that it was an excellent place in which to entertain guests. I was very keen to entertain the people of Kent in the Castle and wanted to

The author, Bunny Connolly-Carew and Keith Bailey at Dover.

foster good relations between the services and the people in the local area. The Castle had been an important part of the County's history and I wanted it to remain an integral part of the community.

On my first inspection of the rooms in my quarters I was struck by a huge lion's head which was emblazoned on the coat of arms over the fireplace in Constable's Tower. Upon closer examination it became apparent that the lion had no whiskers and I felt that this spoiled the look of him somewhat. I duly contacted Whipsnade Zoo and they kindly sent me a set of real lion's whiskers which I put on the lion. They bristled very realistically!

At this time I was fortunate to get an NCO to run the Castle. He was one Keith (Bill) Bailey, whom I knew already as he had looked after at least three Commanding Officers of the 15th/19th Hussars as a batman/driver. Not only was he extremely efficient but over the years he became a great friend. He was an excellent driver and is still with me after thirty-five years. He left the army to come with me when I retired, having just married Wendy Savill, the daughter of the Band Sergeant Major in the Regiment, whom I also knew.

Rather than start their married life in a quarter in Germany Keith preferred a more permanent posting in the UK at Dover. This was due to the fact that he might have been posted to India where there were no married quarters and, having just been married, was not keen to be separated from his wife so soon. I made him a local Sergeant and he set about making Constable's Tower a place renowned for entertainment and organisation. Indeed, there was a fantastic party almost every night and we even had a piper who impressed the guests greatly. Whilst at Dover, I taught him to ride and play polo, squash and tennis. In a very short time he was able to beat me at the latter two!

Sir Robert Menzies was appointed Lord Warden of the Cinque Ports, with a residence at Walmer Castle, at the same time as I arrived at Dover. He was also the Constable of Dover Castle and as Deputy Constable I had much to do with his inauguration. Walmer Castle was small in comparison to Dover, where we had a magnificent dining room, with a refectory table which could seat twenty and shields of past Deputy Constables covering the stone walls. Sir Robert much preferred dining at Constable's Tower and I had endless dinner parties for him in the days leading up to his installation. He was a great authority on dry Martinis, which he insisted on making himself, and after dinner would frequently stay up till about 2 a.m. drinking numerous brandies and reminiscing in a very Churchillian way.

On the night before his installation we held a dinner party for Sir Robert and his wife, Dame Patty, at which the guests included the Archbishop of Canterbury, the Lord Lieutenant, the local MP and the Secretary of State for Defence, plus many of the leading local citizens of Kent. This was a resplendent affair and we even went so far as to engage trumpeters who strode up and down the battlements playing their instruments. Our main problem was in connection with the seating plan as we had so many esteemed guests that we did not know who to sit where! In the end, I had the Archbishop of Canterbury on my left and was so overawed by him that I completely forgot to ask him to say grace at the beginning of the meal. Fortunately, he was very understanding and we said it at the end instead.

All of this imposed a considerable burden on Molly, who

not only had to organise this dinner but all the others, plus all the floral decorations, which were largely provided from the gardens at Bournehill House. My children thoroughly appreciated their time at Dover. My eldest two daughters, Carolyn and Angela, had their coming out dances in the Castle and Robin, who was at school in Kent, had numerous friends to stay. I still have the visitors book and over my three years there we had well over eight hundred guests.

Dover Castle was a convenient port of call for travellers going to and from the continent. Members of my regiment coming back from Germany on leave were frequent visitors and few were the officers who did not spend a night at Constable's Tower. My mother, aged about ninety, was a regular visitor. She was motored down from Warwickshire by one Dr Heather, who looked after her during her later years. They came in an open MG sports car, with scarves and hair flying in the wind. Admiral Begg and Rosemary, his wife, stayed after leaving the Far East and prior to his appointment as Governor to Gibraltar. Molly and I stayed with them in Gibraltar a year or two later. Michael, the Marquess of Reading, and his wife Margot were frequent visitors, together with their children, Alexander and Jacqueline Rufus-Isaacs, who were friends of our children and whom we saw quite a lot of when we were at Bournehill.

David Ennals was the Labour MP for Dover and sometimes his secretary would telephone to say that he would like to call on us at the weekend whilst he was making a constituency visit. On the Friday night he would arrive in his ministerial car, as Minister for the Army, and on Saturday morning he would set off for his constituency office in a rather old and battered Morris. I was lucky in that we were supplied with oil for the central heating and the expenses of all the staff. Harold Wilson, who was the Prime Minister at the time, also authorised an adequate entertainment allowance for me. I think I must have added at least a halfpenny on the income tax over those years!

The first year I was kept busy as GOC 54th Division, visiting units and attending exercises. There were also a large number of evening engagements, as except for my HQ staff, who were mostly regulars, they were all part time territorials. In 1966 Denis Healey reduced the Territorial Army and disbanded my division, so except for a number of training establishments and depots in the south of England, I had few soldiers under command. I was able, therefore, to concentrate on my job as Deputy Constable of Dover Castle and on the inauguration ceremony for the Lord Warden of the Cinque Ports. This took the form of a full dress parade in the courtyard of the Castle, during which we had the ceremony of the handing over of the keys to the Lord Warden. I had the trumpeters of the 15th/19th Hussars on the ramparts of the Castle to sound the fanfare and there was then a service at the Church in the Castle. During the summer the five Cinque Ports entertained the Lord Warden and Molly and I were also invited.

I also started up a polo club on a ground made available by Richard Neame, at Hards Court, and we played most weekends. Altogether a delightful way to finish my career in the army. The only sad thing was that Molly developed a heart disease during the last year and was desperately ill for a least two months. She had to go into hospital in London and although they never really discovered the cause, it was deemed to be due to circulation problems. She just recovered in time to accompany me on a skiing holiday in

Installation of Sir Robert Menzies as Lord Warden of the Cinque Ports.

Kitzbühel, where I broke my leg endeavouring to keep up with my children. Despite the best efforts of Keith to instruct me as to what I should and should not do on the slopes I took off ignoring all advice, shortly to wish that I had listened. Obviously, this put something of a damper on the skiing experience and I spent the rest of the holiday lying on the bed, blowing a hunting horn to get attention, shouting for Martinis and, as Keith informs me, throwing skiing sticks at people when irritated! I had a plate inserted, which kept me on crutches for the next six months.

Whilst at Dover, Keith and Wendy Bailey had their first child, Simon. He was christened in the Chapel and we had a christening party in Constable's Tower. I was a Godfather.

It was in this year that we purchased about ten acres of land on the hill above Monchique in Portugal and decided to build a house there. In those days the amount of money that could be spent abroad was limited but we were greatly assisted by a cousin of Molly's, Douglas Graham, who lived out there and, in fact, sold us the land and lent us the capital to finance it. Molly was always a keen architect, having designed much of the building carried out at Bournehill House. We had the greatest fun drawing up the plans and staking out the measurements on the hill whilst I was still on crutches.

During the next year the house took shape. It was situated on a hill above Monchique, just below Foia Monchique, the highest point in Portugal. We were about 3000 metres up and had a wonderful view over the sea from Cape St Vincent to Albufeira. We were the only house on the hill and had about thirteen acres of land, all terraced. At one time the land had a thriving cultivation of vines which were destroyed by disease in the early part of the century. The

Restolho d'Aveia – house in Portugal.

wild flowers, including peonies and orchids, covered the
hills in the spring and we had eucalyptus, fig, orange and
lemon trees in the garden. We were just about on the tree
line and immediately above us there were no trees at all.
Bird life was rather disappointing, as the Portuguese tended
to shoot everything that flew. However, we had a lot of
nightingales, which were wonderful in the spring and early
summer. We were also frequently visited by the very rare
azure winged magpie. Occasionally we got the golden eagle
soaring above us and it used to nest up at Foia.

We built a swimming pool heated by oil and Molly
immediately set about creating a garden on the two terraces,
which were full of bougainvillaea and other exotic
Mediterranean plants. We installed a generator, which
produced our electricity, and there was reasonable supply of
water on the mountain. Twenty years later, when much of

the mountain had been developed and there were many more houses built, water became a problem.

During 1968 and 1969 Keith Bailey and I motored out on a number of occasions in a Land Rover, to which was attached a horse trailer containing furniture and household goods. It was 1500 miles and we generally stayed two nights along the way, one night in France and the other somewhere near Salamanca in Spain. Later on, when the house was complete, we would fly to Faro and motor up to Monchique in a hired car. It was a wonderful holiday home for the whole family for twenty-three years and we were lucky to have a Portuguese couple, Emanuel and Teresa, to look after us and to cook for us. In fact, it was their departure that led us to the decision to sell, as by then the whole of the Algarve had become rather less attractive.

Keith Bailey, with his wife and son, moved with my wife and me, Nanny, children and dogs, from Dover to Bournehill House: our thirteenth move since our marriage.

CHAPTER 12

Grantham House

BY 1968 BOTH Molly's parents had died and Sedgewick Park had been sold and there were signs that the development at Horsham was going to encroach on our land. Furthermore, owing to what appeared at that time to be the uncertain state of Molly's health following her illness at Dover, we decided to move from Bournehill House, in which I would not wish to live alone. We duly moved to Grantham House in Lincolnshire, an impressive mansion on the east side of Grantham, which had belonged to the Sedgwicks, relations of my mother. Mr Sedgwick had purchased the house in the mid nineteenth century, developed Alzheimer's disease in about 1880 and was despatched to an asylum. In those days they did not understand this disease and this was, I believe, the normal practice. He had two daughters, Marion and Winifred, who never married, believing themselves to have tainted blood.

I knew the house well and with my family had stayed there on average once a year for the past forty-eight years. I now own the visitors book I mentioned earlier in which the first two entries are of the Reverend W.R. Wyldbore-Smith and Miss Dorothy Green and it was the occasion when my mother and father became engaged. Grantham House, with 28 acres, is one of the oldest substantial houses in the town. It was originally a country residence but, as time went by, the beautiful town of Grantham was built up around it. I found it to be a lovely place to live and was soon an accepted part of society owing to my keen interest in hunting, shooting and fishing.

The house was built in the middle of the fourteenth century and was once known as Hall Place, having been named after the Hall family who lived here from the end of the fourteenth century until the beginning of the seventeenth. They were a family of wool merchants from Calais. The entire house and the present group of outbuildings including the church are of stone, probably brought to Grantham from the Ancaster quarry nearby with mainly Collyweston tiled roofs. The house was originally the open hall type, dating from about 1350, and to this period belongs the central hall.

The house was bought by Sir Richard Cust in 1734 and was the Cust family home for over two centuries. It became the dower house of the Belton Estate during this time. The Cust family modernised the house so that it was in keeping with the time, added a new staircase, put the ceiling in the hall and created three attic rooms above. The asymmetrical entrance dates back to 1574 and was added to in 1737 and it is this kind of amalgam of styles and eras which gives the house its architectural distinction.

The inside of the house also reflects this diverse and interesting history. The oak wainscot in the panelled room was inserted in the early seventeenth century whilst the painted panelling in the drawing room was created almost a hundred years later. I feel that this was probably under the direction of Lady Cust who was responsible for bringing in the three large still life paintings by J.B. Ruoppolo. These fine works of art are believed to have come from Belton

Hall, a house lying in north Grantham and a residence which Lady Cust was later to inherit.

The house was a very important historical location and, in years gone by, Margaret Tudor, daughter of Henry VII, stayed here for a time as she journeyed to Scotland to meet her husband, James IV of Scotland. Cardinal Wolsey, who was also journeying northwards, stayed here too.

After the war, in about 1949, the Sedgwicks made the whole property over to the National Trust, in view of the fact that they had no children and were unmarried. They left a proviso in the will of Marion Sedgwick, the last living daughter, that on their death the tenancy of the house should be offered first to my brother and then to myself. My brother was not interested in it and I therefore accepted it with some delight! I agreed with the National Trust to modernise it – installing electricity and central heating and redecorating throughout. The cost was about £20,000 and in return Molly and I would live in the house rent free. We were to take responsibility for the grounds and the house interior whilst the National Trust were to be responsible for any outside or structural repairs. Through our partnership with the National Trust we were very happy to have visitors at the house and received approximately 50 per year. They seemed to take great pleasure in wandering round the extensive grounds and taking in the visual delights of Molly's newly transformed garden.

Indeed, the garden was one of the real gems of Grantham House and all Molly's hard work and enthusiasm paid off. After some time the garden was transformed totally. The kitchen garden had previously been covered in grass and many trees had had to be taken down because they were unsafe. However, we brought down some of our own trees

Grantham House: the author with his dogs.

from Horsham which had to be carried by a firm of experts. They must have looked rather strange and I remember passing them during the journey down here. Eventually the garden began to resemble a traditional medieval paradise, boasting cedars, acers, walnut, catalpa, aralis, pawlonia and liliodendren all complemented by a rockery pool, a vegetable patch and a not so medieval tennis court.

The garden was certainly a beauty and its charm was further enhanced by the view across the River Witham and Sedgewick Meadows. Though the house was actually very close to the town it had all the appeal of a country dwelling, largely due to the vast meadows stretching out at the rear of the house.

The move from Bournehill House to Grantham House was finally made after we had gradually transported the contents of the former during the summer. There was a cottage in the courtyard which Keith Bailey occupied with his family, which was shortly to be increased by the birth of another son, Timothy, on 28 December. He was born in the cottage with the assistance of Molly, as his arrival beat that of the arrival of the ambulance.

CHAPTER 13

Brief Business Interlude

WHEN I LEFT DOVER in 1968 I did a short business course in London. When my military career finally came to an end I felt that a logical next step would be to go into business but was soon to discover that my talents did not lie in this particular area. I remember being taught something about how to buy and sell products, a form of pyramid selling. I was encouraged to purchase several hundred bottles of 'Swipe' cleaning agent, the idea being to sell them on to another businessman and thereby make a profit. This scheme did not turn out quite the way I planned and a great many bottles of 'Swipe' linger on in Grantham House to this day!

After my unsuccessful attempts to sell cleaning products I thought I would branch out in another area of business. As I had started working at Central Office I spent Monday to Friday in London and was only in Grantham over the weekend. I therefore decided to start a restaurant at Grantham House and serve dinners on four days a week, Thursday, Friday, Saturday and Sunday. We served the meals in the elegant Grantham dining room which had a maximum of eight tables. I got a licence to serve alcohol with meals and brought in my chef from Dover, Ray Harrison, setting him up in a house in Grantham. Keith Bailey was head waiter, with his wife Wendy acting as waitress. It was slow to develop but on Fridays and

Saturdays we usually got bookings for about four or five tables. We treated the customers in the restaurant very much as if they were guests at a sophisticated dinner soirée and the tables were lavishly decorated with silver and candelabras.

Ray Harrison was an excellent chef, but highly extravagant. Food was ordered in bulk and only the best meat and fish provided. The inhabitants of Grantham were rather surprised to find the new owners of Grantham House eating in the restaurant and Molly and I lived extremely well at weekends when we were there. However we were frequently confronted with Dover sole, partridge and other unconsumed food, which we were quite unable to deal with. Eventually the food bills run up by the chef far outstripped any profits we were making for the limited number of dinners and after a year I decided to give it up. We were getting fatter and fatter and poorer and poorer – something which could not continue indefinitely! Ray Harrison left us to go to the Earl and Countess of Gainsborough, who had much admired his culinary skills when dining with us. After a few years they also found his expensive shopping more than they could withstand and he left them to go to Glamis Castle, to work for Micky Glamis. Now the Earl of Strathmore, he was a good friend of my son Robin whilst at Eton. Presumably he has greater financial means to enable him to accommodate his extravagant chef!

My next effort at running a business was to take over a long established 'corner shop', situated next to Grantham House and opposite the King's school, on the retirement of its owner, Mr Cave. It was sold to me with the promise of amazing income from the local schoolchildren. What Mr Cave did not instruct me in was how to manage the many children who would crowd into the shop at the beginning and end of each day. The shop had an excellent turnover but on my monthly stock check I was puzzled to find that although I was selling vast numbers of sweets we were losing money heavily. On investigation I discovered that the boys had worked out a drill where a few of the older, more mature, scholars would divert the manageress, a very attractive young lady, whilst the smaller boys filled their pockets with sweets. I therefore decided that I would be better off working for the Conservative Party and gave up my last effort at running a business. When looking back on this time in my life I feel that the only real lesson I learned was that I should never attempt to run a business again!

CHAPTER 14

A Career in Politics

ON 5 MAY 1968 I finally retired from the Army after thirty-five years. I had given little thought to what I intended to do on retirement but at one of our last dinner parties at Dover, Lord Carrington, who I think was then Chairman of the Conservative Party, was a guest and he asked me what I intended to do. I told him I had no fixed ideas and he asked me if I would like to come and help him over the next six months to raise money for the Conservative Party from the business sector; they needed a million pounds.

The money to fund the Conservative Party came from the constituencies but they found that not enough money could be raised in this way. Each constituency had a quota and around £1 million was needed to fund the party each year. Although less was spent at this time it became clear that the method was ineffectual and new means were called for. It was for this reason that the party turned to business and this proved to be an infinitely more successful way of raising party funds. Despite the fact that the quota never altered we raised more and more money each year owing to the new methods we employed.

I had known Peter Carrington in a personal rather than a work-related capacity and it was because we got on well together rather than because he thought I had any particular talent for fund-raising that he asked me to work with him.

In politics you deal with a different breed: frequently pleasant people and sometimes highly intelligent. Their interests lay in maintaining their positions as Members of Parliament or Ministers, at the expense of others, if necessary. It was a much more static life, in that it was not necessary to move house from year to year and I was more integrated into civilian society.

I said I would be delighted to help and later in the year I went around the City of London with him and visited many businesses, both in London and elsewhere. He knew a vast number of businessmen and had great prestige. This was a new aspect of life for me and very different to areas in which I had previously been involved. Though the job was not political in nature and merely involved obtaining necessary funds for the party to survive, we did have contact with the politicians and my knowledge of this area also increased. I knew very little either about politics or about business and the whole experience was to be a great learning curve for me. My early days in the job mainly involved keeping quiet and listening to what was being said, learning what methods were employed and how the negotiations were handled. We would visit three or four companies each day with varying degrees of success.

The response from most of the Chairmen was positive, partly due to the fact that Peter knew many of them in a social context, and we raised the one million pounds. Not only this but I learned a great deal about the obtaining of political donations and enjoyed this new occupation immensely. Later we aimed to raise much larger amounts and in the second year we raised £3 million whilst in my final year in the job we managed to accumulate a huge £10 million.

These monies had to be obtained from private individuals and businesses rather than from the trade unions which supported the Labour party. We approached industrial companies and Peter's contacts helped greatly to prepare the ground. Sometimes, however, we were fobbed off with secretaries but the majority of the time we gained access to the Chairman of the company.

In 1969, largely as a result of the period with Peter Carrington, Lord Chelmer, then Treasurer of the Conservative Party, asked me if I would become a permanent member of the Conservative Board of Finance. I was intrigued by what I had seen of the political life and readily agreed. And so I began my second career, at the age of fifty-five, earning £1,400 per annum!

At this time, 1970, 80 per cent of the men who had achieved great things in business had themselves been involved in National Service and this provided me with a tactical procedure for obtaining funds. I felt that if the chairmen, most of whom had a great respect for the army as they had been involved in it themselves, were approached by others who had held esteemed positions in the military, they would be more likely to support our cause and give generously. Consequently, I engaged a number of retired officers to assist in the fund-raising for the party. This proved to be immensely successful and the majority of chairmen agreed to see us as they had a great respect for the Brigadiers and Major Generals who approached them. They had a certain amount of regard for senior officers; at least they were honest and motivated by their cause. Also, having army pensions they would not require such a high salary.

We had a representative in eleven different areas of Britain and each one would liaise with the most successful businesses in the area. This too proved to be a good system and one which was very effective. As well as approaching the English businesses we also concentrated upon wealthy individuals who lived abroad but who had business interests in this country. If having a Conservative government was going to benefit their business then they would be more likely to donate to the party funds. A great deal of money came from Hong Kong which was still a British colony at this time. This was to draw the wrath of the Labour party but I felt that their logic in protesting against our methods was somewhat twisted. They, after all, were supported by the trade unions who had an interest in having a Labour government and I personally thought that this was very fair. Why then, did they object to the Conservatives gaining funds from those whose interests we protected?

Though there were many press reports to the contrary, we employed no underhand methods in gaining money from Conservative supporters. If someone had an interest in the party then they could legitimately offer their support by the donation of finances. Additionally, if someone was being examined by the Scrutiny Committee for a Knighthood or similar honour they would be immediately discounted. There were a great many accusations that certain people had paid for their knighthoods. Asil Nadir was one such individual and there was much controversy surrounding this matter.

There were, however, some great scandals taking place whilst I was fund-raising. One of the most infamous and impacting was Cecil Parkinson's affair with Sarah Keys. This proved to be an unpleasant shadow which hung over the Blackpool conference that year. The news of the affair broke on the final day of the conference and dominated the newspapers totally and utterly. I felt rather aggrieved at this as Margaret Thatcher's speech was splendid but was not reported in the press because of the voracious interest in Cecil Parkinson's involvement with Sarah Keys.

Parkinson was forced to resign when news of the affair hit the headlines and I personally felt that this was a great shame. I liked Cecil Parkinson very much – he was a nice chap and good at his job. That he had chosen to have an affair may not have been the most admirable thing to do but this surely should have been a private matter between him and his wife. It certainly bore no relation to his ability to do his job and the whole business only tarnished the Conservative Party and deprived them of a perfectly good chairman.

Working for the Conservative Party provided me with a very different way of life. The family was now living at Grantham House and I also had a flat in London so that I could stay there when I was working during the week. I knew just what I would be doing from day to day – a stark contrast to army life – and was, to all intents and purposes, my own master. Though I had a room in Conservative Central Office I kept away from the politicians as I had little interest in their job and it would have been unethical from them to have meddled in mine. Additionally, I was in very close contact with No. 10 Downing Street and worked quite closely with the Prime Minister. It was a challenge I relished and from which I learned a great deal.

During my time working for the Conservative party I spent a substantial amount of time with the party chairmen and treasurers. Most of these men were very competent professionals who acted with gravitas and dignity whilst others were not so good at their jobs. For example, Alistair

McAlpine was an excellent treasurer but his successor, Lord Beaverbrook, was not so good at the job. He eventually went bankrupt himself and had to cease being a treasurer. Party treasurers nominated their own successors to be chosen by the Prime Minister and I am inclined to believe that they often nominated someone who they felt would be terrible at the job, just to make themselves look better.

In contrast to figures like Alistair McAlpine and Ian Gow, some prominent politicians were not nearly so good at their chosen professions. Chris Pattern was, in my opinion, one such individual. When I first started working for the party he was a young researcher at Central Office. I did not find him to be a charismatic or effective individual but nevertheless he worked his way through the party ranks. He had such animosity towards the treasurer's department that he eventually destroyed it and had the politicians take over the fund-raising. This came as a great shock and went against everything we had done in the past, having made a great effort to keep the two separate. It also made the donations scheme seem very sleazy and the new methods made it seem as though the party was accepting funds from disreputable and corrupt sources when this was not actually the case.

I am rather saddened by the turn politics has taken in recent years. In days gone by politicians used to be men of stature who took up this challenging occupation because of their firmly held beliefs. Now I believe that many modern politicians are simply in it for the money, something which would have been unheard of in the earlier days. My father-in-law, for instance, was a successful businessman involved in shipping. He was deeply committed to improving the state of the country and entered politics because of this. Indeed, he could not have gone into this area for the money and he received only £700 per annum for his efforts. This, in my view at least, was a good thing and prevented the House of Commons from being flooded by career opportunists as it seems to be now.

In 1974 it paradoxically became much easier to raise funds as the Conservative Party had just lost an election. The businessmen were afraid that they would be penalised by a lengthy stay in power by the Labour government and were much more inclined to help with our fund-raising than they had been in previous years. I also received much more support from the newly appointed Margaret Thatcher and her Treasurer Alistair McAlpine than I had from her predecessor, Ted Heath.

Ted Heath was a man of whom I had not been particularly fond and I felt that Margaret Thatcher made a much better Prime Minister. I do recall having some pleasant conversations with him in Bucks' Club but these were largely to do with his hobby, sailing, rather than with political matters.

One particular incident stands out in my memory. It was after the 1974 election, which we had lost, and I had organised a grand dinner to which I invited all those who had made generous donations to the party. At the end of the dinner Ted Heath was to make a speech in which he would thank all these donors for their financial backing and try to rouse the party spirit after the defeat. He arrived at the dinner in an absolutely foul mood and hardly said one word to anyone for the duration of the meal. When he had finished dining he got up and left without uttering a syllable of gratitude to any donors at all. Though he was obviously upset at having lost the election, it did not help to have behaved in this way and this was something that his successor would never have done.

Whilst the Party was in opposition, it was comparatively easy to raise funds to get rid of the existing Labour government. Later on, when we were in power, it became more difficult. I set up about four Industrial Councils around the country, which were run by my representatives and whose members comprised the leading industrialists in each area. The role of these Councils was to meet several times during the year, generally with a cabinet minister present. At these meetings they could present their views on various aspects of current policy. They then acted as fund raising agents for the party.

In the run-up to the 1970 election, one of these Industrial Councils held a dinner in Manchester, at which Edward Heath and Lord Carrington, the then Party Chairman, were present. In view of the importance of this meeting, I also attended. We had about forty potential donors from industry present.

After the dinner we had to run Lord Carrington back to his hotel and I drove him in my car with Edward Heath, accompanied by Lord Chelmer. Back at the hotel we had a drink with Lord Carrington and I then returned with the other two to the place where we were staying. Unfortunately, on the way back I went the wrong way down a one way street and was stopped by the police. When they saw us all in evening dress I was breath tested and found to be positive. As soon as we were stopped, Edward Heath jumped out of the back of the car and walked off, but Lord Chelmer stayed with me while we went to the police station, where I had a blood test. Meanwhile, Keith Bailey had been sent for and he motored us all back to the hotel. As a result of this unfortunate incident I lost my licence for a year. However, Lord Chelmer gave me great support and it had little effect on me as I was driven everywhere by Keith.

In 1974, in the midst of the economic depression and the winter of discontent, Edward Heath called an election. Unfortunately the timing was wrong and we lost it. Again in the autumn there was another election which we lost by a narrow margin. As a result of this, Margaret Thatcher took over the leadership of the Party from Edward Heath.

CHAPTER 15

Margaret Thatcher and Me

WORKING FOR Margaret Thatcher was very different from serving under Edward Heath. She brought in Alistair McAlpine, a young businessman aged about twenty-eight, as Assistant Treasurer and he soon replaced Lord Chelmer. Margaret Thatcher had a very forceful personality and it was rather like serving under Montgomery! She and Alistair McAlpine were a powerful combination. He had a very wide acquaintance with many leaders of industry and was extremely persuasive. Margaret Thatcher gave us every support by holding receptions for industrialists at Number Ten and meeting anyone whom Alistair produced.

I spent about three days a week in London at Central Office in Smith Square and also had an office in Grantham, where Keith Bailey's wife, Wendy, became my secretary and remained so for fifteen years.

In 1979 Margaret Thatcher became our first woman Prime Minister and life became very interesting. The next ten years were among the most exciting of my career. Mrs Thatcher was like a breath of fresh air into a party which was rapidly becoming stale. As with General Montgomery, people have asked me whether Margaret Thatcher was a 'nice' person and the answer, once again, would have to be no. She too had many good qualities and was a woman I admired very much and esteemed greatly. She was both fair and kind and had a wonderful sincerity which is rarely

Margaret Thatcher at Grantham House.

found amongst modern politicians. Yet she could also be ruthless and critical.

I found that if you performed your job correctly then you had no reason to fear or dislike her but if she discovered that you were resting on your laurels then you would encounter her 'iron lady' persona. He best features included an ability to get the people on side, which she demonstrated during the Falklands War whilst her worst character trait was probably an inability to relax. My own relationship with her was excellent and I recall her showing her softer side when I was ill with cancer. She telephoned my family after I had had an operation and was very concerned about my health and well-being.

Mrs Thatcher was also very loyal to those people with whom she enjoyed a close relationship and I remember her being deeply distressed when her former PPS, Ian Gow, was brutally murdered by the IRA. Similarly, she gave her total support to Peter Carrington who resigned at the commencement of the Falklands War. He was Defence Secretary at this time and felt that he had failed in his role by allowing the Falkland Islands to be taken. Rather than criticise and apportion blame, Margaret Thatcher gave him her full backing and did not want him to resign but to stay in the job. In a crisis such as this she was completely unflappable and it was the hard times during which her wonderful leadership qualities really came into play. However, I recall her getting into a great panic when her son Mark was lost in the desert, so much so, in fact, that she despatched her husband to go and find him!

Politically too Mrs Thatcher was a force to be reckoned with. She was responsible for Britain's victory during the Falklands War, confronted the power of the trade unions in the infamous miners' strike, reduced the influence of local government by abolishing metropolitan councils and introduced the largely unpopular poll tax. She was a politician of real ability and acumen and would not tolerate disobedience or subordination, from the opposition or her own party.

The Labour Party seemed to visibly shrink and quiver under her gaze. Her force and zest left them in total disarray and forced them to think about their policies and the best way to put them across more carefully. Conversely, the Conservatives were immeasurably strengthened under her leadership and after her appointment as leader in 1975 the Party went from strength to strength. Though her rise to leadership of the Party was unexpected it was by no means undeserved and I personally feel that she was the very best person for the job.

Her first year in office saw the Falklands War. I shall never forget a morning in October 1983, during the Falklands Campaign, going round to Number Ten to see Ian Gow, who was then her PPS, about some matter. I found the Chiefs of Staff outside the door to Number Ten, waiting to see the Prime Minister for their daily briefing. They included John Nott, the Secretary of State for Defence, who had been a company commander in Malaya, when I commanded the 15th/19th Hussars at Ipoh, and whom I knew well. There was also General Dwin Bramall, the CIGS, who had been on my staff as a GSO1 in Singapore and Admiral Henry Leach, the Chief of the Naval Staff, who had also been on my staff in Singapore. I could not resist greeting them with, 'Stand at ease, gentlemen.'

Her second term of office was marked by the miners' strike. This ended when she defeated the miners and the balance of power shifted away from the trade unions and towards the government. As ever, Mrs Thatcher remained stoical and firm, even in the face of criticism, and acted in the way she thought was best, adhering to her principles and maintaining her genuine sincerity.

The party conferences were always a great highlight of the political term and were held in Brighton, Blackpool or Bournemouth. These would last for four days and I would write to some of the leading industrialists and ask them to attend. We had many lunches, dinners and social occasions and the events were very much a leisure activity. The chairmen of the major companies would attend and we would all bring our wives along. We had an excellent time and these conferences were also very beneficial. The highlight would be the speech given by Margaret Thatcher on the closing day. She was a truly marvellous orator, the like of which has not been seen for some time. Whilst Tony Blair, a man of some ability, tries to emulate her sincerity, William Hague is sincere yet lacks her political acumen.

CHAPTER 16

The Brighton Bombing

IN OCTOBER 1984 we were at the Grand Hotel in Brighton and on Thursday, the last night before the final session on Friday morning, when the Prime Minister gives the main address, I retired to bed at about midnight. I was in Room 625, overlooking the front. It was a twin room as Molly normally accompanied me. However, she was unwell so missed what must have been her only conference in twenty years. This was to prove to be an incredibly lucky twist of fate.

I soon drifted off to sleep but my slumber was to be disrupted in the most dramatic and unpleasant way. A mighty flash of light and an appalling explosion suddenly awakened me. I looked around and saw that the bed nearest the window was completely covered in shattered glass; this was the bed in which Molly would have been sleeping. The whole room was full of acrid smoke and I could hear the sound of falling masonry outside. Though the scene I surveyed was terrible destruction I remained calm. I suppose that my lengthy military career had helped me cope with this situation and, despite the blast having caught me off guard, I retained my wits. I opened the door and to my right, in the haze, I could see a gap the whole way down, where the staircase had been. To my left the passage seemed intact.

I quickly put on some clothes over my pyjamas and some shoes, gathered my belongings and found my way to a fire escape which led to the back of the hotel. I had known instantly that this terrific explosion must have been caused by a bomb and my first thought was to leave the building as quickly as possible. Shadowy figures, some in pyjamas and some dressed, accompanied me and I made my way to the beach at the front of the hotel. Looking back I could see that the whole of the foyer had disappeared and there was a gap from floor to roof where the stairs and lift had been. Fire engines and ambulances were racing up and the police had cordoned off the area. I came across Keith Joseph in his dressing gown and we wondered what had become of the Prime Minister and Denis Thatcher. Fortunately, it was a lovely warm evening and after about an hour the police came round and said that those who wished could move into the Metropole next door. I was certainly very impressed with the way everyone seemed to cope with this horrendous disaster and, though there were some casualties, the bombing was not as bad as it might have been.

I then saw Alistair McAlpine, who told me that the Prime Minister was safe, although her suite had been badly damaged. He said he had arranged for Marks and Spencers to open at 6 a.m. to provide clothing for those who needed it, so that the final session of the conference could go ahead as planned. Before moving into the Metropole, the last thing I saw was a stretcher being lowered down the front of the Grand. On it was Norman Tebbit, covered in rubble. His wife also sustained horrific injuries in the blast and remains paralysed as a result of the events of that terrible night.

I had been in the Metropole for about half an hour when the loudspeaker system announced that everyone must vacate the building immediately, as there was a suspected bomb in the vestibule. I had just had time to telephone

Molly at Grantham to tell her that I was all right and I then moved out again into a bed and breakfast establishment next door.

I said earlier that I have been lucky in life: never more so than on that night! It was later discovered that the bomb had been placed in the water cistern of Room 627, next door to me, and that the blast had been vertical, which was why I had had the narrow escape. It transpired that it had been planted by the IRA some weeks previous to its explosion and that it was operated by a timer and designed to explode during the party conference.

The bomb was planted by Patrick Magee, a member of the IRA who wanted to assassinate the Prime Minister and her whole cabinet. At his sentencing the judge said, 'You intended to wipe out a large part of the government and you nearly did.'

I and the other guests in the hotel were unspeakably glad that he had not succeeded but were still grieved by the unnecessary loss of life and the injuries some of our party had sustained. We found that Magee had checked into the hotel under the fictitious name of Roy Walsh a few weeks before the commencement of the conference. His stay lasted from 14 to 17 September and he primed a 20-lb bomb in the room he was occupying, setting it to detonate during the conference. Magee had apparently learned something of explosives whilst associating with terrorists in Libya.

Though the results of this despicable act were not as tragic as they might have been, five people lost their lives in the explosion: Sir Anthony Berry, the MP for Enfield Southgate; Roberta Wakeham; Eric Taylor, the North West Area Chairman; Muriel Maclean; and Jeanne Shattock. The three women were wives of Conservative ministers and had attended the conference socially. Their deaths could not possibly have furthered the cause of the IRA and this somehow makes the bombing all the more sickening.

The police investigations were extensive and they questioned and eliminated around eight hundred people from fifty different countries from their list of possible suspects. These people had all been staying in the hotel in the month before the Conservative Party conference. There was only one man who could not be accounted for – Roy Walsh. Eventually, the elusive Roy Walsh was identified as Patrick Magee. This was thanks to a palm print on his hotel registration card which matched the print of Patrick Magee who had been arrested three years earlier in Norwich, where he spent his childhood. He was finally arrested and jailed but showed no remorse for his crimes, giving a clenched fist salute when he was sentenced.

I did not attend the trial of the man who had killed my colleagues and nearly succeeded in killing me too. Obviously I felt much compassion for the relatives and friends of those who had lost their lives in the blast and was pleased that justice was done when Magee was sentenced but did not really have any strong feelings about the whole affair. I had become used to unknown enemies making attempts on my life and felt that I had had more than one lucky escape.

The bombings, assassinations and attempts on people's lives were, paradoxically, quite good for the Party. It ensured that we had public opinion on our side and the whole country seemed to surge forward in a tide of defence against the IRA. We were also able to bounce back from these disasters fairly quickly and, apart from the obvious loss of life, the bombing did not do us much harm at all and served to unify the Party rather than to damage it.

At 10 a.m. on the Friday, the Conference Hall, about fifty yards further along the front, was packed, as the Prime Minister arose to announce that terrorists would not deter the Conservative Party. This was greeted with tremendous applause. She also imparted to her audience the sad news that four people were known at that time to have been killed and several injured.

The usual planned industrialists' lunch had to make way for sandwiches and canapés, which were distributed to the guests in their seats. I think they appreciated this more than a four-course lunch. Sir John King was amongst those industrialists present and he very kindly gave me a lift back to Grantham that afternoon in his private aircraft. I had no problems with luggage, as it remained in Room 625; it was later returned to me.

The IRA were very active during the 1980s and the police obtained a list of prominent political figures who were in danger of being assassinated. I myself appeared on one such list owing to my involvement in raising funds for the Party. This did not really worry me too much as I had faced much worse and more immediate dangers when I was fighting in the Second World War. I also believed that I was not terribly high up on the list and that it would be quite some time before the IRA attacked me. Despite this, my close friend and driver, Keith Bailey, had to take an advanced drivers' course where he was taught how to swerve and turn to avoid disasters in the road and how to check for bombs under the bonnet and the wings of the car.

Ian Gow was just one of the people who fell victim to the ruthless determination of the IRA. He had been Margaret

Thatcher's PPS and she was devastated when he was killed. Ian Gow was unceasing in his loyalty to the Prime Minister and totally devoted to the Anglo-Irish cause. He was a man who truly enjoyed life and work and had a great ability to laugh. I was deeply shocked when he was killed and felt we had lost a charming man and a talented politician.

However, my chief memories of Ian Gow are happy ones and I vividly recall him having a real passion for White Ladies. A great cricketer, he would sometimes demand that a White Lady be brought to him during the game! I also knew his lovely wife, Jane, and attended their wedding. His selfless side was displayed when, as a lawyer, he represented soldiers who were being court-martialled for minor offences. He was sorely missed by all the Conservative Party, Margaret Thatcher in particular.

CHAPTER 17

Political Vignettes

MUCH OF MY TIME as Director of the Conservative Board of Finance was spent travelling around visiting the Representatives in their areas and attending fund raising functions. In 1986 I held a dinner at Grantham House with about twelve of the local industrialists present. As usual, we had a prominent politician or senior party official to make the appeal and on this occasion, Jeffrey Archer, the then Deputy Chairman of the Party, came down from London to take on this role.

The guests were having drinks before dinner when the telephone rang and someone asked to speak to Jeffrey Archer. He took the call in my study and after a short time came back and said to me, 'Do you mind if I make the appeal at the beginning of dinner rather than at the end, as something has cropped up which necessitates me returning to London as soon as possible?' He made the appeal and then left. The next morning one of the tabloid newspapers printed the story of how he had purportedly paid a prostitute £2000 for her favours. He immediately resigned as Deputy Chairman of the party. This was after spending only one year at Conservative Central Office.

Jeffrey Archer said in court that he had never even met this woman but had arranged for a friend of his to give her the £2000 to prevent her from fabricating a scandal about the high profile politician. He told the jury that he had made himself look a fool but that he was not a liar before being awarded a colossal £500,000 in libel damages which he nobly gave away to charity.

However, the story, sadly for Mr Archer, did not end there and his very public recent trial saw the high profile politician and prolific author jailed for four years in one of the most serious perjury cases of the modern era.

I travelled fairly extensively in search of funds, especially to Hong Kong, where there were a number of prominent and fairly successful businessmen who had substantial business interests in England and who were eager to get a Conservative Government. They made no secret of their support and I seldom returned without substantial cheques for the Party. One person who was extremely helpful to me at that time was C.H. Tung, who hosted a number of events for me and provided several useful introductions. Now, Chief Executive of a Hong Kong under Chinese control, he would probably prefer to forget this!

In 1986 Algy Cluff and I flew out to Hong Kong to raise funds for the Party. Algy Cluff was an SAS member and had been with me in Borneo when I was Chief of Staff there. I got on very well with him and had kept in touch with him after leaving the army. Molly and I would frequently go and visit him and his family in Dover. He had married a very beautiful and intelligent woman called Blondel whose parents were from Anguilla in the West Indies. This was in a time when mixed race couplings were not always looked upon kindly but it was obvious to everyone what a charming couple they were. Algy went into mining and has success-fully run both gold and platinum mines. He later developed a new metal called niobium and is one of the most prosperous businessmen I have known.

When we were in Hong Kong C.H. Tung, a leading industrialist out there, organised a dinner party for a number of potential supporters, including Li Ka-Shing and Sir Y.K. Pao. I had an appointment to visit the Chairman of the Hong Kong and Shanghai Bank on the morning of our arrival. Unfortunately the flight was delayed and I had to motor direct from the airport to his office. He was so impressed that I think he agreed to a donation on the spot.

Algy Cluff had extensive oil interests at that time and he was invaluable at drumming up support. I never understood why Margaret Thatcher did not appoint him as Treasurer when Alistair McAlpine resigned in 1990. Instead, at the instigation of Alistair, Lord Beaverbrook was appointed. He was not a success and left in 1992.

In the 1987 election there were fears during the last week that support was dwindling and, in consequence, about £3m was spent on advertisements during the last ten days. There were no prizes for second place during an election and it would have been unthinkable for the Treasurers to be in a position where they could limit expenditure and thus perhaps lose two or three vital seats.

Allegations of political influence being sought by donors became rife and at the beginning of the 1990s there was uproar in the press, encouraged by the Labour Party. On 22 June they tabled a motion in the House of Commons on the subject of political fund raising. During this time innuendo and rumour abounded concerning donations from individuals who had at some stage acted illegally. In previous years it would have been the responsibility of the Treasurers to answer such press claims but now the Party Chairman was actively involved and the whole principle of the confidentiality of private donations was questioned. Instead of a robust statement to the effect that donors, like voters, were entitled to keep their political affiliations secret, every excuse was made and politicians even failed to insist that people who lived abroad and who had a sympathy with and investments in this country would have the right to support the party of their choice.

One major scandal involved the infamous businessman Asil Nadir, formerly Chairman of Polypeck. The Conservative Party accepted a donation of around £100,000 from his company and, though he was later proved to be one of the less scrupulous business moguls, we were not aware of this at the time of accepting the donation, which was perfectly legitimate. The whole business struck me as being similar to the experiences of the Labour Party with Robert Maxwell as they did not know he too was unscrupulous when he supported them. However, a great fuss was made about the Nadir incident which was most unfortunate.

In 1989, Ian Gow, then Minister for Housing, previously Margaret Thatcher's PPS and who had great influence with her, was blown up by the IRA. They planted a bomb in his car outside his house in Sussex which killed him instantly. This was an absolute tragedy and was one of the reasons why Margaret Thatcher was unseated in 1990; he would never have allowed her to go to Paris on that vital day when the votes were being cast.

I retired as Director of the Conservative Board of Finance in 1992, after the election, which we had just won. I wrote to the Treasurer who succeeded Alistair McAlpine, one Charles Hambro:

> During the last week I have been bombarded with requests for interviews by Channel 4, Radio 4, ITV and the Select Committee. I have supported the Central Office

Memorandum to the Select Committee and have given an interview to ITV, in conjunction with Alistair McAlpine, in which I hope I have reflected the official line that the present system of fund raising is satisfactory and have endeavoured to refute some of the widely inaccurate statements that have been appearing in the press.

However, as a result of my twenty-two years experience as Director of the Conservative Board of Finance, I do have two strong views, which so far I have not mentioned. Firstly, the fund raising for the Conservative Party should be in the hands of the Treasurers and politicians should not be involved. This was the practice up until 1990 and, in consequence, the accusations now rife that donors, both private and corporate, have political influence is thus avoided. We never involved either Ted Heath or Margaret Thatcher, when they were Prime Ministers, in fund raising functions, other than receptions which were open to all supporters of the Party.

If a donor wished to hand a cheque to them it was handed to a Treasurer in their presence. Secondly, the Treasurers exercised no control over the spending. This was, quite rightly, left to the Party Chairman. In consequence, over several years, expenditure exceeded income by a large amount. To avoid this I always advocated there should be trustees of the Party funds, consisting of elder statesmen and not current members of the Government or shadow ministers, for example, William Whitelaw, Alec Douglas-Home etc, who would have the power to prevent overspending by the current leaders of the Party. In 1977 I did manage to establish a capital fund which was meant to build up a reserve on which only the interest was available. This, needless to say, was a failure, and was spent by the Party at the next election. Obviously in the present circumstances, this is not practical until the overdraft is paid

off but it might prevent a similar situation in the future. I
hope these thoughts may be of some use to you. With best
wishes.

The financing of political parties depends on voluntary
contributions, either corporate or personal. The alternative
is state funding which, at present, is not acceptable to any of
the political parties. It was clear that the Conservative Party
received its support from corporate and personal donations
from those who favoured a Conservative government. The
Labour Party received much of their support from trade
unions, who quite reasonably thought their interests were
best served by a Labour government. I never understood
why the Conservative Party should attack the Labour Party
for receiving support from unions, any more than the
Conservative Party should be criticised for receiving support
from industry. If company chairmen believe that Conservative policies best serve their interests they have every right to
pledge their financial support.

During my period as Director, I travelled endlessly,
visiting Representatives in every area about once a month. I
think that Keith Bailey and I must have covered more than
20,000 miles a year by car. Each Representative kept a record
of the money raised in his area and there was a strong
competitive spirit. During the twenty-three years in my
capacity as Director we raised £121 million.

Later on the Labour Party launched a campaign designed
to discourage our corporate and, indeed, our private, donors,
some of whom lived abroad. In particular, they criticised our
donations from Hong Kong. They completely failed to
realise that people like the late Sir Y.K. Pao and Li Ka-Shing
had more money invested in this country than many of our

largest donors. As Algy Cluff pointed out in an article in the *Spectator*, 'Sir Y.K. Pao's companies had supported the British Shipbuilding Industry for many years and there are many working men for whom Mr Kinnock professed to speak at that time who had more to thank Sir Y.K. Pao for than they had Mr Kinnock.'

Another line of attack by the Labour Party was that large donors were rewarded with knighthoods. The chairmen of large and successful companies, who probably owed their success to Conservative policies, received recognition for their success in business and it is interesting to note that three of the leading Conservative supporters at that time received knighthoods from the Labour Party, who, quite rightly, recognised their achievements. These were James Hanson, John King and James Goldsmith. Any name which we put up for an honour was always investigated by the Honours Scrutiny Committee and one thing that was quite certain to go against any award being given was if it was discovered the candidate had made a large donation to the Conservative Party. One wonders what on earth has happened nowadays, when large donors to the Labour Party are openly given peerages.

Fund raising was the responsibility of the Treasurers and Ministers and Members of the Cabinet were not included in any fund raising negotiations with donors. They did not know, in fact, who the donors were, as corporate political donations were only declared in company accounts in the year following the donation. Probably once a month Alistair McAlpine would see the Party Chairman and tell him how much money there was. Otherwise no politician would know anything about the fund raising activities. If a donor wished to make a donation personally to the Prime Minister it was done in the presence of the Treasurer and the cheque was handed to the Treasurer and not to the Prime Minister.

In 1991, shortly after Chris Patten was made the Chairman of the Party, it was felt by the politicians that the Prime Minister should not deal with the Treasurers but that they should come under the Party Chairman, who himself would take part in fund raising activities. The Chairman would organise direct mailing and he would see individual donors. This immediately involved politicians with fund raising. I regard this development as largely the fault of Chris Patten, who managed not only to destroy the fund raising machinery of the Conservative Party but, some years later, the Royal Ulster Constabulary as well, in his 'Patten Report' to the Labour Government.

CHAPTER 18

An Active Retirement

IN 1969 I HAD started hunting with the Duke of Rutland's hounds, known as the 'Belvoir Hunt', and in 1970 was asked to become Joint Master with Sir John King, later Lord King of Wartnaby. In those days the Hunt Master was responsible for the financial running of the Hunt, assisted by a small grant from the committee. It cost about £30,000 a year to run a Hunt, about £8000 of which was normally provided by the committee. Being Master of Foxhounds was therefore a very expensive pastime. However, my family did, at least, hunt free! Shortly afterwards, it became so expensive that the committee had to meet the whole expenditure and the Masters acted as agents for the committee. John King had been an MFH for many years and I learnt a great deal from him. He became a great friend of mine and I was a great admirer of his.

Having spent thirty-five years in the army, moving around the world, it might have been a problem settling in Grantham House in Lincolnshire, an old county whose inhabitants are somewhat insular and rather reserved. However, I had known it all my life and had stayed at the house with my parents probably at least once a year. I was greatly helped when I became MFH of the Belvoir. In this capacity I saw a good deal of Charles Rutland and his wife Frances. I had, in fact, known her mother as Margaret Whigham, when I was in the deb circuit in the 1930s, when I first joined the army.

I was able to provide some of the money required because my mother had died and left me a bequest in her will which enabled me to carry on as Joint Master for three years. I knew that it would have given her great pleasure to know that I had spent it in this manner. Of my children, two daughters and one son hunted, so in the holidays I had the pleasure of being accompanied by Penelope, Nicola and Robin.

By 1970 we were well installed at Grantham. Before moving I had mixed feelings about leaving Bournehill but any doubts I harboured were soon alleviated by the splendour of Grantham House. Being involved in the hunt helped me settle in and I soon made lots of good friends in the area. My wife and children were also pleased with the area and we were soon very much at home here. Molly had set about creating what was to become a garden of some renown. We had moved about thirty specimen trees and shrubs from Bournehill when we left.

In 1970 I was appointed Colonel of the 15th/19th Hussars, an appointment which is normally held for seven years. I was responsible among other things for providing suitable young officers for the Regiment and had to attend functions such as annual regimental parades, to visit the regiment at least twice a year and to undertake any other tasks to improve and help the morale of the Regiment. The 15th/19th Hussars had always been a regiment which prided itself on the standard of its officers, not necessarily for their military successes but for their ability to get on with each other and with the soldiers under their command.

With this in mind, I concentrated on finding young men who had finished their schooling and were interested in a career in the army. If I considered them to be suitable candidates, I arranged for them to spend a week with the Regiment, to see how they got along with the other officers and how they enjoyed the general atmosphere of the Regiment. I used to put three or four of them into my Land Rover and with Keith Bailey, would motor them to wherever the Regiment was at that time, usually in Germany, but on one or two occasions in Northern Ireland.

After a week of living in the mess and taking part in a number of military functions taking place at that time, I would bring them back and if they had been approved by the Regiment and were themselves favourably impressed, I would set the wheels in motion to get them started on their army careers. This proved very successful and almost all of those who entered this way had a good career, either as regulars or on short service commissions, and at least four of them eventually came to command the Regiment. We were affiliated to the Northumberland Hussars, a Territorial armoured car regiment. Many of our officers joined this unit, which was situated in our recruiting area of Durham and Northumberland, when they retired from the regular army.

I attended many of their military parades and a number of their summer camps. Whilst I was Colonel, HRH Princess Margaret was appointed Honorary Colonel of the 15th/19th Hussars. She attended our annual officers' dinner and also visited the Regiment, wherever it was, at least once a year. On these occasions I had to be present. Molly also had a role during this time and was always present when wives were included.

As well as the Duke of Rutland, there was another local family who made us welcome – the Welbys. Their family had lived at Denton Manor, near Grantham, for well over four hundred years and they owned about twenty thousand acres. Sir Oliver Welby and his wife Barbara asked me to shoot soon after we arrived, and later Sir Bruno Welby and his wife Jane were equally kind to us. I shot with them on many occasions and also, latterly, with their son, Charles Welby, who worked for me in the Conservative Board of Finance.

Margaret Thatcher had now established her Foundation at 36 Chesham Place and after I retired from the Conservative Board of Finance in 1992, she asked me to join the Thatcher Foundation, in order to raise funds. This was an organisation which had been established in 1991 in order to provide a wider understanding of the principles central to free enterprise both in Britain and America. It has given support to those training in the fields of business and law and I was happy to be a part of it.

It was a fascinating job and although not a full time occupation, I had to travel around a considerable amount. This also entailed visiting London at least once a week and I continued doing this until 1998. This was an excellent way of winding down after a full and somewhat hectic career. It involved raising money for a college at Cambridge and only took up four days of my time each week. Thus I was kept occupied whilst simultaneously being able to enjoy the pleasures retirement had to offer. My previous experiences with fund raising for the Conservative Party helped enormously and we raised the £2 million target easily.

I became a Governor of the King's School in the Eighties and was Chairman of the Board until about 1995. I knew Derek Lee, the headmaster, socially and he requested that I join the Board of Governors. This I enjoyed enormously, as the school is one of the leading grammar schools in the country, where Isaac Newton was educated. It has a magnificent record, educationally, in sports, historically and architecturally. Situated immediately opposite Grantham House, I have always taken the greatest interest in it. The boys at the school were smart, well disciplined, polite and very helpful and I had the utmost respect for the headmaster and the way he ran the school. Grammar schools of this kind came under threat during my period as a Governor but we managed to save the school and it remains a Grammar School to this day.

I had given up hunting when I reached seventy-eight years and although I continued to ride and still kept two of my hunters, I put my efforts into shooting. In addition to the Welbys, Lyonel Tollemache of Buckminster frequently invited me to go shooting and I also had a gun with Adrian Massingberd-Mundy at his shoot at Somerby for over fifteen years.

Lord Belper of Kingston always gave me several days each season and in 1980 I was shooting there and John King was one of the guns. I remember one lunchtime he was telephoned by Number 10 (Downing Street) by Margaret Thatcher asking him to take over British Airways, which was losing money heavily at that time. At the end of the day John King gave me a lift to London in his Range Rover and we discussed the pros and cons of taking on the task. He was in no doubt as to the problems he would face and the many economies he would have to introduce – no more free flights for all the directors' families and relations! We had dinner at the Dorchester when we got to London. In those days I had a room there, thanks to Alistair McAlpine, whose family owned the hotel. The next day John King went to see Norman Tebbit, then Chairman of the Party, and accepted the job. Within a very short time he had completely restored British Airways.

I was over eighty years old when my involvement with the Thatcher Foundation eventually ceased, and was now ready to slow down and take life at a more leisurely pace. The last few years represent a period in my life which I have enjoyed very much. I take great pleasure in my very comfortable home and also in the gardens which my wife has spent so long cultivating and nurturing. Rather than pursuing such active hobbies I now enjoy reading and am very fond of biographies in particular. I borrow a great many books from my good friend John King who has similar taste to me.

I am also a proud grandfather and have eight grand-children. I find that there are great differences between them and my own children, all of whom were privately educated, and often wonder which generation will fare better in the ever-changing modern world. Whilst my daughters concentrated upon raising their families my son made business his first priority but my grandchildren have not followed this same pattern.

Carolyn's children attended comprehensive schools and rarely saw their father during the impressionable teenage years. They spent a great deal of time with their friends indulging in modern pursuits, and are very street-wise. However, they do not seem to have suffered from this upbringing and all now have successful careers which they pursued straight after leaving school. The other grand-children were educated privately and enjoyed the luxury of two-parent families – something increasingly rare in today's society. They have all had gap years after leaving school and lack the street-wise nature of their cousins, but I have no doubt that all will be successful at whatever it is they decide to do.

Conclusions

As I SIT IN THE STUDY at Grantham House, looking back over the past eighty years, I am amazed at the change in the way of life that has taken place. Of course, eighty years is a mere fraction of the period during which Grantham House has existed. In the early days the plague was rampant in East Anglia, Cromwell, who originated from the Fens, was in power and the Smith family was unheard of in these parts.

Nevertheless, there has been a radical change in the last eighty years. I have seen the advent of the internal combustion engine and electricity, social development, political correctness and the litigious society which has developed from it, threatening especially the efficiency of our armed forces. I am greatly saddened by the destruction of the House of Lords and the development of the professional politician. No longer do men and women of stature and character, who have achieved success in other spheres, enter politics. The House of Commons is now filled with ex social workers, civil servants, second class lawyers and teachers. A democracy deserves the Government it elects, so the lowering of all our standards must be due to the attitude of voters. This is partly due to urbanisation, decrease in rural influence, the arrival of migrants from ethnic minorities with no pride in the nation, a lack of discipline and the breakdown of family life; unlike the average married couple today, Molly and I have been happily married for fifty-six years.

I have already remarked on the luck that has attended me over the past eighty-seven years. Perhaps the greatest stroke of luck was to have been born in 1913 rather than in the year 2000!

Further Reflections

THROUGHOUT THESE memoirs I have emphasised how lucky I have been on a number of occasions. I even considered giving them the title 'Memoirs of a Lucky Major General'. However since completing them I have been faced with a very different situation.

My wife has suffered a fatal stroke, my only son has died aged forty-three and now the terrorist attacks on America have resulted in the most appalling loss of life – all in the last three months. Perhaps I should have been born five years earlier.